LangServe

A Hands-on Guide to Deploying AI with LangChain

Charles Sprinter

LangServe: A Hands-on Guide to Deploying AI with LangChain

Table of Contents

Chapter 1: Introduction to LangServe and LangChain

1.1 What is LangServe?

LangServe is a powerful deployment tool designed specifically for applications built using **LangChain**, a framework for creating AI-driven systems with chains of prompts, tools, and models. LangServe simplifies the process of turning LangChain prototypes into production-ready services by enabling developers to deploy them as scalable RESTful APIs.

Key Features of LangServe:

1. **Schema Inference**: Automatically generates input and output schemas, reducing manual configuration effort.

2. **API Endpoints**: Supports features like batch processing, streaming, and invocation of LangChain workflows via REST APIs.

3. **Monitoring Tools**: Integrates seamlessly with LangSmith for tracing and debugging.

4. **High Performance**: Optimized for handling concurrent requests, making it suitable for high-traffic environments.

1.2 The Role of LangChain in AI Application Development

LangChain provides the building blocks for developing AI-powered workflows by chaining together:

- **Prompts**: Predefined or dynamically generated instructions for large language models (LLMs).

- **Tools**: Functions or APIs to perform specific tasks, such as retrieving information from databases or generating code.

- **Memory**: Context management to maintain conversation history or workflow state.

- **Models**: Large language models (e.g., OpenAI GPT, Anthropic Claude) and others.

Developers often use LangChain to:

- Create chatbots.

- Automate knowledge retrieval.

- Perform sentiment analysis on text data.

- Process real-time data streams.

However, while LangChain excels at prototyping, deploying these workflows to production poses challenges. This is where **LangServe** plays a crucial role by bridging the gap between development and deployment.

1.3 Why LangServe?

The Challenge: From Prototype to Production

AI developers often struggle to move their LangChain applications from local prototypes to production environments due to:

- **Complex Deployment**: Setting up APIs and managing infrastructure can be time-consuming.

- **Scaling Issues**: Handling multiple requests and ensuring high availability often require expertise in server management.

- **Monitoring and Debugging**: Lack of robust tools to monitor performance and trace issues in real time.

The Solution: LangServe

LangServe solves these problems by providing:

- **Simplified Deployment**: Automatically wraps LangChain workflows into APIs, requiring minimal configuration.

- **Scalability**: Optimized for handling concurrent requests efficiently.

- **Integrated Monitoring**: Built-in support for LangSmith ensures developers can trace and debug workflows seamlessly.

- **Faster Time-to-Market**: Developers can focus on improving their applications rather than managing complex deployment pipelines.

1.4 Real-World Applications of LangServe

LangServe is highly versatile and can be applied across industries to deploy AI applications efficiently:

1. Customer Support Automation

- **Use Case**: Deploy chatbots to handle customer queries.

- **Example**: A chatbot API integrated with an e-commerce website to assist users in finding products and resolving common issues.

2. Knowledge Management Systems

- **Use Case**: Build a document retrieval API to search across a large corpus of knowledge.

- **Example**: A corporate intranet search tool for employees to retrieve policies and reports.

3. Real-Time Sentiment Analysis

- **Use Case**: Analyze customer feedback in real-time from social media platforms.

- **Example**: A streaming API deployed with LangServe to process and classify tweets by sentiment.

4. Personalized Recommendations

- **Use Case**: Provide tailored product or content recommendations.

- **Example**: A recommendation engine deployed as a LangServe API for a streaming service.

5. Healthcare Information Retrieval

- **Use Case**: Aid healthcare professionals by retrieving relevant medical information.

- **Example**: A knowledge retrieval system for doctors to access treatment protocols or research papers.

1.5 Overview of the Book

This book, **"LangServe in Action: A Hands-on Guide to Deploying AI with LangChain"**, is designed to provide you with everything you need to master LangServe and deploy LangChain applications seamlessly.

What You Will Learn

1. **Foundational Concepts**:

   o   Basics of LangServe and LangChain.

   o   API deployment fundamentals.

2. **Practical Projects**:

   o   Deploy chatbots, sentiment analysis tools, and document retrieval systems.

   o   Real-world case studies to illustrate LangServe's capabilities.

3. **Advanced Features**:

   o   Scaling applications for high-performance use cases.

   o   Configuring LangServe for security, customization, and monitoring.

4. **Best Practices**:

   o   Debugging and optimization techniques.

   o   Cost-efficient deployment strategies.

5. **Future Trends**:

   o   The evolving landscape of AI deployment and the role of LangServe.

How This Book is Structured

- **Part I: Introduction and Foundations**: Lays the groundwork with an overview of LangServe, LangChain, and their applications.

- **Part II: LangServe Basics**: Covers the step-by-step process of deploying your first LangChain application.

- **Part III: Advanced Features**: Explores advanced deployment techniques, monitoring, and security.

- **Part IV: Use Cases and Projects**: Walks you through practical projects and real-world examples.

- **Part V: Optimization and Best Practices**: Focuses on debugging, scaling, and cost management.

- **Part VI: Appendices and Resources**: Provides additional reference materials, tools, and learning resources.

Code Example: Deploying a Simple LangChain Application with LangServe

python

```python
from langchain import PromptTemplate, LLMChain
from langserve import serve


# Define a simple LangChain application
prompt = PromptTemplate(input_variables=["name"],
template="Hello, {name}! How can I assist you?")
```

```
chain = LLMChain(prompt_template=prompt,
llm="openai-gpt3")


# Deploy the LangChain application using
LangServe
if __name__ == "__main__":

    # Start the LangServe server

    serve(chain)
```

Explanation of Code

- **PromptTemplate**: Defines a template for interacting with the user.

- **LLMChain**: Chains the template with an LLM (e.g., OpenAI GPT-3).

- **serve**: Deploys the application as an API using LangServe.

Running the Code

1. Save the script as simple_langserve.py.

2. Run the script using python simple_langserve.py.

3. Access the deployed API endpoint at http://localhost:8000/invoke.

LangServe is a critical tool for developers looking to transition their LangChain applications from experimental prototypes to scalable production systems. This book will guide you step-by-step, ensuring you gain both theoretical knowledge and practical skills to leverage LangServe effectively.

Chapter 2: Getting Started with LangServe

2.1 System Requirements and Prerequisites

To successfully use LangServe, ensure your system meets the necessary requirements. These requirements are straightforward but crucial for a seamless experience.

Hardware Requirements:

- **Processor**: A multi-core processor (Intel i5 or equivalent and above is recommended)

- **Memory**: At least 8 GB of RAM (16 GB or more recommended for large-scale applications)

- **Disk Space**: 2 GB of free disk space for LangServe installation and dependencies

Software Requirements:

- **Operating System**:

    o Windows 10/11, macOS 10.15 or later, or Linux distributions such as Ubuntu 20.04+

- **Python**:

    o Version 3.8 or higher. Use python --version to check your Python version.

- **Package Manager**:

    ◦ pip or conda for installing Python packages. Verify with pip --version.

Additional Tools:

- **Git**: For cloning repositories and version control.

- **cURL or Postman**: To test API endpoints.

- **Docker (optional)**: For containerized deployment of LangServe.

Prerequisite Knowledge:

- Familiarity with Python programming

- Basic understanding of REST APIs

- Experience with LangChain (optional but helpful)

2.2 Installing LangServe

LangServe can be installed easily via Python's package manager pip. Follow the steps below to get started.

Step 1: Install Python

1. Download Python 3.8+ from the official Python website.

2. During installation, ensure "Add Python to PATH" is selected.

Step 2: Set Up a Virtual Environment

A virtual environment keeps your project dependencies isolated.

bash

```
# Create a virtual environment
python -m venv langserve_env


# Activate the environment
# On Windows:
langserve_env\Scripts\activate
# On macOS/Linux:
source langserve_env/bin/activate
```

Step 3: Install LangServe

Use pip to install LangServe and LangChain:

bash

```
pip install langserve langchain
```

Step 4: Verify Installation

Check if LangServe is installed successfully:

bash

```
python -m langserve --version
```

```
If the installation was successful, this command
outputs the installed version of LangServe.
```

2.3 Understanding LangServe's Architecture

LangServe simplifies the deployment of LangChain applications by wrapping them into RESTful APIs. Here's an overview of its architecture:

Core Components:

- **LangChain Object**:

    o The workflow or application you've developed using LangChain.

- **LangServe Engine**:

    o Automatically converts your LangChain object into RESTful APIs.

- **Endpoints**:

    o /invoke: Executes the LangChain workflow.

    o /batch: Processes multiple requests in parallel.

    o /stream: Streams responses for real-time applications.

Workflow:

1. **Developer Input**: Create a LangChain object.

2. **LangServe Configuration**: Pass the object to LangServe.

3. **API Deployment**: LangServe generates RESTful endpoints.

4. **External Access**: APIs are consumed by external applications.

This architecture abstracts complex deployment processes, allowing developers to focus on building workflows rather than managing infrastructure.

2.4 Key Components and Terminology

Understanding LangServe's terminology will make the deployment process clearer.

Term	Definition
LangChain	A framework for creating workflows using prompts, models, and tools.
Schema	Defines the structure of input and output data for an API endpoint.
Endpoint	A specific API route for invoking workflows, e.g., /invoke.
Streaming	Incrementally processes and sends data to the client as it's generated.
Concurrency	The ability to handle multiple requests simultaneously.
LangSmith	A monitoring and debugging tool that integrates with LangServe for observability.

2.5 Running Your First LangServe Application

Follow this step-by-step guide to deploy your first LangServe application.

Step 1: Create a Simple LangChain Workflow

Here's an example of a basic LangChain application:

python

```python
from langchain import PromptTemplate, LLMChain
from langserve import serve


# Define a prompt template
prompt = PromptTemplate(input_variables=["name"],
template="Hello {name}, welcome to LangServe!")


# Create a LangChain object
chain = LLMChain(prompt_template=prompt,
llm="openai-gpt3")


# Serve the LangChain object
if __name__ == "__main__":
    serve(chain)
```

Step 2: Run the Application

1. Save the script as app.py.

2. Execute the script:

bash

```bash
python app.py
```

3. LangServe will start a server at http://localhost:8000.

Step 3: Test the API

Use cURL or Postman to test the API:

bash

```
curl -X POST http://localhost:8000/invoke \
    -H "Content-Type: application/json" \
    -d '{"name": "Alice"}'
```

Expected Response:

json

```
{
  "response": "Hello Alice, welcome to
LangServe!"
}
```

Step 4: Debugging Errors

If the API doesn't work as expected:

- Check for typos in your code.

- Ensure LangServe and LangChain are installed properly.

- Look at the terminal logs for error messages.

By following these steps, you've successfully deployed your first LangChain application using LangServe. This foundational setup will serve as the basis for more complex deployments covered in later chapters.

Chapter 3: Building APIs with LangServe

3.1 RESTful APIs

APIs, or **Application Programming Interfaces**, allow different software systems to communicate with each other. A **RESTful API** (Representational State Transfer API) is a widely used architectural style for building web services. It uses standard HTTP methods to perform operations like creating, reading, updating, and deleting data.

Key Principles of RESTful APIs:

1. **Stateless**:

    o Each request from a client to a server must contain all necessary information. The server does not store client context between requests.

2. **Resources**:

    o Data or functionality exposed by the API is treated as a resource, identified by a URL.

3. **HTTP Methods**:

    o GET: Retrieve data.

    o POST: Send data or create a resource.

    o PUT: Update an existing resource.

    o DELETE: Remove a resource.

4. **Data Formats**:

   ○ REST APIs typically use JSON for request and response payloads.

Why Use RESTful APIs?

- Easy to implement and integrate.

- Compatible with web-based applications.

- Scalable and widely supported.

LangServe utilizes RESTful principles to expose LangChain workflows as accessible endpoints, making it easy to integrate AI capabilities into web and mobile applications.

3.2 Automatic Schema Inference: How LangServe Handles Input/Output Schemas

When deploying a LangChain application, understanding the format of input data (requests) and output data (responses) is essential. LangServe simplifies this process through **automatic schema inference**.

How Schema Inference Works:

1. **Input Analysis**:

   ○ LangServe examines the LangChain workflow's expected input variables.

   ○ It automatically generates a schema (data structure) describing the required fields.

2. **Output Prediction**:

   ○ Based on the LangChain logic, LangServe predicts and structures the output format.

3. **Documentation**:

   ○ LangServe provides a detailed schema accessible via a metadata endpoint, allowing developers to understand the required data structure.

Example: Simple Input/Output Schema

Consider the following LangChain application:

python

```python
from langchain import PromptTemplate, LLMChain
from langserve import serve


# Define a prompt template
prompt = PromptTemplate(input_variables=["name"],
template="Hello {name}, how can I help you
today?")
chain = LLMChain(prompt_template=prompt,
llm="openai-gpt3")


# Serve the chain
if __name__ == "__main__":
    serve(chain)
```

Automatically Inferred Schema:

- **Input Schema**:

Json2

```
{
  "name": "string"
}
```

- **Output Schema**:

json

```
{
  "response": "string"
}
```

Benefits of Automatic Schema Inference:

- Reduces manual effort in defining data formats.

- Ensures consistency between input and output.

- Minimizes errors during API consumption.

3.3 Working with /invoke, /batch, and /stream Endpoints

LangServe provides three main types of endpoints for interacting with LangChain workflows.

/invoke: Standard Request-Response Endpoint

- Used for single requests.

- Processes the input and returns a single response.

- Example Request:

bash

```
curl -X POST http://localhost:8000/invoke \
    -H "Content-Type: application/json" \
    -d '{"name": "Alice"}'
Example Response:
json


{
  "response": "Hello Alice, how can I help you today?"
}
```

/batch: Batch Processing Endpoint

- Processes multiple requests simultaneously.

- Ideal for batch operations to save time and resources.

- Example Request:

bash

```
curl -X POST http://localhost:8000/batch \
    -H "Content-Type: application/json" \
```

-d '[{"name": "Alice"}, {"name": "Bob"}]'

- Example Response:

json

```
[

  {"response": "Hello Alice, how can I help you
today?"},

  {"response": "Hello Bob, how can I help you
today?"}

]
```

/stream: Streaming Endpoint

- Streams the response incrementally as it is generated.

- Useful for real-time data or long responses.

- Example Request:

bash

```
curl -X POST http://localhost:8000/stream \

    -H "Content-Type: application/json" \

    -d '{"name": "Charlie"}'
```

- Example Response:

bash

Hello

Charlie,

how

can

I

help

you

today?

Endpoint Comparison Table:

Endpoint	Use Case	Advantages	Example
/invoke	Single requests	Simple and straightforward	Chatbots, FAQs
/batch	Multiple simultaneous requests	Saves processing time for bulk data	Bulk sentiment analysis
/stream	Real-time or large responses	Reduces wait time for results	Real-time stock price updates

3.4 Example: Creating a Simple REST API for LangChain Applications

This example demonstrates how to create and deploy a REST API for a LangChain application using LangServe.

Step 1: Create the LangChain Application

python

```python
from langchain import PromptTemplate, LLMChain
from langserve import serve


# Define a prompt template
prompt = PromptTemplate(
    input_variables=["name"],
    template="Hi {name}, welcome to our AI-powered service!"
)


# Create a LangChain workflow
chain = LLMChain(prompt_template=prompt,
llm="openai-gpt3")


# Serve the workflow as an API
if __name__ == "__main__":
    serve(chain)
```

Step 2: Save the Script

- Save the script as simple_api.py.

Step 3: Run the LangServe Server

bash

```bash
python simple_api.py
```

Step 4: Test the API

- Use a tool like Postman or curl to test the /invoke endpoint:

bash

```bash
curl -X POST http://localhost:8000/invoke \
    -H "Content-Type: application/json" \
    -d '{"name": "John"}'
```

Response:

json

```json
{

  "response": "Hi John, welcome to our AI-powered
service!"

}
```

Step 5: Test Batch and Stream Endpoints

- Batch:

bash

```bash
curl -X POST http://localhost:8000/batch \
    -H "Content-Type: application/json" \
    -d '[{"name": "John"}, {"name": "Jane"}]'
```

Response:

json

```
[

   {"response": "Hi John, welcome to our AI-
powered service!"},

   {"response": "Hi Jane, welcome to our AI-
powered service!"}

]
```

- Stream:

bash

```
curl -X POST http://localhost:8000/stream \

    -H "Content-Type: application/json" \

    -d '{"name": "Alice"}'
```

Response (streamed):

css

Hi

Alice,

welcome

to

our

AI-powered

service!

By the end of this chapter, you have:

- Learned the basics of RESTful APIs.

- Understood how LangServe handles schemas automatically.

- Explored the main LangServe endpoints.

- Created a fully functional REST API for a LangChain application.

Chapter 4: Deploying Your First LangChain Application

4.1 Preparing a LangChain Application for Deployment

Before deploying a LangChain application using LangServe, it's important to structure and test the application locally to ensure smooth deployment.

Key Steps to Prepare:

1. **Define the Workflow**:

   o   Use LangChain components (e.g., prompts, chains, tools) to create a clear workflow.

   o   Ensure the workflow solves a specific problem, such as answering questions or performing calculations.

2. **Verify Dependencies**:

   o   Ensure all required Python libraries (LangChain, LangServe, etc.) are installed.

   o   Use the requirements.txt file to list dependencies for consistency:

text

```
langchain>=0.1.0

langserve>=0.1.0

openai>=0.10.2
```

  o Install dependencies:

bash

```
pip install -r requirements.txt
```

3. **Test the Application**:

  o Test the LangChain application in a local environment before deployment.

  o Example Test Script:

python

```
from langchain import PromptTemplate, LLMChain


# Define the prompt template
prompt = PromptTemplate(input_variables=["name"],
template="Hello {name}, how can I assist you?")
chain = LLMChain(prompt_template=prompt,
llm="openai-gpt3")


# Test the chain
result = chain.run(name="Alice")
print(result)
```

4. **Plan Input/Output Schema**:

  o Document the expected inputs and outputs for the workflow.

  o Example:

- Input: {"name": "string"}

- Output: {"response": "string"}

4.2 Configuring LangServe Settings

LangServe provides flexible settings to customize the deployment of your LangChain application.

Key Configuration Options:

1. **Port Configuration**:

   o Specify the port on which LangServe runs. By default, it uses 8000.

   o Example:

bash

```
python app.py --port 8080
```

2. **Environment Variables**:

   o Use environment variables to manage sensitive information (e.g., API keys).

   o Example .env file:

text

OPENAI_API_KEY=your_openai_api_key

3. **Logging**:

o   Enable logging to monitor application activity and debug issues.

o   Example configuration:

bash

```
python app.py --log-level debug
```

4. **Concurrency Settings**:

o   Adjust settings to handle multiple requests simultaneously:

▪   Example:

bash

```
python app.py --workers 4
```

Configuration Example:

Assume you want to deploy your application on port 8080 with 4 workers and debug-level logging:

bash

```
python app.py --port 8080 --workers 4 --log-level debug
```

4.3 Deploying a Basic Conversational Agent

Step 1: Create the LangChain Application

This example demonstrates deploying a conversational agent that greets users.

python

```python
from langchain import PromptTemplate, LLMChain
from langserve import serve


# Define the prompt template
prompt = PromptTemplate(
    input_variables=["name"],
    template="Hello {name}, welcome to our
service! How can I help you today?"
)


# Create the LangChain workflow
chain = LLMChain(prompt_template=prompt,
llm="openai-gpt3")


# Serve the LangChain workflow
if __name__ == "__main__":
    serve(chain)
```

Step 2: Save the Script

- Save the above code as chat_agent.py.

Step 3: Run the LangServe Server

bash

```
python chat_agent.py
```

Step 4: Test the Deployment

- Use curl to test the API:

bash

```
curl -X POST http://localhost:8000/invoke \
    -H "Content-Type: application/json" \
    -d '{"name": "Alice"}'
```

Response:

json

```
{

  "response": "Hello Alice, welcome to our
service! How can I help you today?"

}
```

Step 5: Integrate the API

- Use the API endpoint in your web or mobile application for user interaction.

4.4 Debugging Deployment Issues: Common Errors and Fixes

Deployments can encounter issues. Below are common problems and their solutions:

Error	Cause	Solution
ModuleNotFoundError	Missing	Ensure all dependencies

Error	Cause	Solution
	dependency	are installed. Run pip install -r requirements.txt.
Invalid API Key	Incorrect or missing API key for LLMs (e.g., OpenAI)	Verify the .env file and ensure the correct API key is used.
Address already in use	The specified port is already in use	Use a different port by running the script with --port <new_port>.
Timeout Error	Workflow takes too long to process	Optimize the LangChain logic or increase timeout settings in the client.
Schema validation failed	Input data does not match the expected schema	Verify the input data format. Use the metadata endpoint to check the required input/output schema.
Server crashes with no error log	Insufficient memory or CPU resources	Reduce concurrency settings or run the application on a more capable machine.
CORS Policy Error	Cross-origin requests blocked when consuming the API from a	Configure CORS headers in the API client to allow cross-origin requests.

Error	Cause	Solution
	browser	

Debugging Tools:

- **Logs**:

  o Enable debug logs during server execution for detailed error tracing:

bash

```
python chat_agent.py --log-level debug
```

- **Postman**:

  o Use Postman to simulate and test API requests with detailed error feedback.

- **LangSmith Integration**:

  o Enable LangSmith tracing for real-time debugging:

bash

```
python chat_agent.py --enable-tracing
```

Example: Resolving a Schema Validation Error

1. Check the schema using the metadata endpoint:

bash

```
curl http://localhost:8000/metadata
```

Response:

json

```json
{
  "input_schema": {
    "name": "string"
  },
  "output_schema": {
    "response": "string"
  }
}
```

2. Adjust the input to match the schema:

bash

```bash
curl -X POST http://localhost:8000/invoke \
    -H "Content-Type: application/json" \
    -d '{"name": "Bob"}'
```

By following these steps, you can confidently deploy a LangChain application, troubleshoot issues, and ensure smooth operation for your users. This foundational knowledge prepares you for building more complex LangServe deployments in later chapters.

Chapter 5: Scaling LangServe Applications

5.1 Understanding Concurrency and Scalability

Scaling is essential when your application must handle increasing traffic or complex workloads. Two key concepts are critical to understanding scalability:

Concurrency

- Concurrency refers to the ability of a system to handle multiple tasks simultaneously.

- In LangServe, this means processing multiple API requests in parallel without degrading performance.

- A concurrent system effectively manages resources (CPU, memory) to minimize wait times and maximize throughput.

Scalability

- Scalability is the ability of a system to handle growth efficiently by upgrading resources or optimizing architecture.

- LangServe supports both **vertical scaling** (adding more power to the server) and **horizontal scaling** (adding more servers or processes).

Term	Definition
Throughput	The number of requests processed per second.

Term	Definition
Latency	The time taken to process a single request from start to finish.
Bottleneck	A point where the system slows down due to resource limitations.

Understanding these terms will help configure LangServe effectively for high performance.

5.2 Configuring LangServe for High Performance

LangServe provides several options to optimize performance and handle higher traffic. Below are key configurations:

Worker Processes

- LangServe uses multiple worker processes to handle concurrent requests.

- By default, the number of workers is set based on the CPU cores available.

- To manually configure workers:

bash

```
python app.py --workers 4
```

Port Configuration

- Each LangServe instance runs on a single port. For large deployments, you can start multiple instances on different ports and use load balancing.

bash

```
python app.py --port 8001
python app.py --port 8002
```

Request Timeout

- Set a timeout to terminate requests that exceed the expected processing time:

bash

```
python app.py --timeout 30
```

Asynchronous Processing

- LangServe supports asynchronous workflows for tasks that do not require immediate responses.

- Example:

python

```
from langchain import PromptTemplate, LLMChain
from langserve import serve


prompt = PromptTemplate(input_variables=["name"],
template="Hello {name}, processing
asynchronously!")

chain = LLMChain(prompt_template=prompt,
llm="openai-gpt3")
```

```
if __name__ == "__main__":

    serve(chain, async_mode=True)
```

Logging and Monitoring

- Enable logging to track performance issues.

bash

```
python app.py --log-level debug
```

5.3 Load Balancing and Handling Multiple Concurrent Requests

For high-traffic applications, implementing load balancing ensures stability and optimal performance.

What is Load Balancing?

- Load balancing distributes incoming traffic across multiple servers or instances to prevent overloading any single resource.

- Benefits:

    o Ensures high availability.

    o Reduces latency during peak traffic.

    o Improves fault tolerance.

Techniques for Load Balancing with LangServe

1. **Round Robin**:

   o Distributes requests equally among all available instances.

   o Example: Deploying LangServe on ports 8000, 8001, and 8002:

bash

```
python app.py --port 8000
python app.py --port 8001
python app.py --port 8002
```

2. **Weighted Load Balancing**:

   o Assigns weights to instances based on their capacity.

   o Example: Assigning more weight to an instance running on a server with higher CPU power.

3. **Auto-Scaling**:

   o Automatically adds or removes instances based on traffic.

   o Use cloud platforms like AWS or GCP for auto-scaling.

Using a Load Balancer

To implement load balancing, you can use tools like **NGINX**. Below is a configuration example for NGINX as a load balancer:

nginx

```
http {

    upstream langserve_backend {

        server localhost:8000;

        server localhost:8001;

        server localhost:8002;

    }


    server {

        listen 80;


        location / {

            proxy_pass http://langserve_backend;

        }

    }

}
```

Testing Load Balancing

1. Deploy LangServe instances on ports 8000, 8001, and 8002.

2. Configure NGINX with the above settings.

3. Test the setup by sending requests:

bash

```bash
curl -X POST http://localhost/invoke \
    -H "Content-Type: application/json" \
    -d '{"name": "Alice"}'
```

5.4 Example: Deploying a High-Traffic Chatbot API

Objective

Deploy a chatbot API capable of handling thousands of concurrent requests.

Step 1: Define the Chatbot Application

Create a chatbot application in chatbot.py:

python

```python
from langchain import PromptTemplate, LLMChain
from langserve import serve


# Define the chatbot prompt template
prompt = PromptTemplate(
    input_variables=["user_input"],
    template="User: {user_input}\nBot: I am here
to assist you!"
)
```

```python
# Create the LangChain workflow
chain = LLMChain(prompt_template=prompt,
llm="openai-gpt3")


# Serve the chatbot application
if __name__ == "__main__":
    serve(chain)
```

Step 2: Start Multiple Instances

Run multiple instances of the chatbot on different ports:

bash

```bash
python chatbot.py --port 8000 --workers 2
python chatbot.py --port 8001 --workers 2
```

Step 3: Configure Load Balancer

Use NGINX as the load balancer to distribute traffic:

1. Add the following to your NGINX configuration:

nginx

```nginx
upstream chatbot_backend {
    server localhost:8000;
    server localhost:8001;
}


server {
```

```
listen 8080;

location / {

    proxy_pass http://chatbot_backend;

}

}
```

2. Restart NGINX:

bash

```
sudo systemctl restart nginx
```

Step 4: Test the High-Traffic Setup

Simulate high traffic using tools like **Apache Benchmark**:

bash

```
ab -n 1000 -c 100 http://localhost:8080/invoke
```

- -n 1000: Total number of requests.

- -c 100: Number of concurrent requests.

Step 5: Monitor Performance

Monitor the API's performance using:

- Logs: Analyze LangServe logs for bottlenecks.

- LangSmith: Use tracing to identify latency issues.

Expected Output

1. Response to individual requests:

json

```
{

    "response": "User: How can I assist
you?\nBot: I am here to assist you!"

}
```

2. Load test results:

   o High throughput and low latency.

   o Even distribution of requests across instances.

By configuring LangServe for concurrency, leveraging load balancing, and optimizing settings, you can deploy scalable applications capable of handling high traffic effectively. This knowledge equips you to build robust, production-ready AI systems.

Chapter 6: Monitoring and Observability

6.1 Introduction to LangSmith and Its Integration with LangServe

Monitoring and observability are crucial for ensuring the reliability and performance of AI applications deployed with LangServe. **LangSmith**, a dedicated tool in the LangChain ecosystem, enables real-time monitoring, logging, and debugging for LangChain applications.

Key Features of LangSmith:

1. **Tracing**:

   o   Tracks the flow of requests through the LangChain workflow.

   o   Visualizes how prompts, tools, and outputs interact.

2. **Logging**:

   o   Captures detailed logs of workflow execution.

   o   Helps identify errors, bottlenecks, and inefficiencies.

3. **Performance Metrics**:

   o   Measures latency, throughput, and error rates.

   o   Provides insights into application health.

Benefits of LangSmith Integration:

- Provides a centralized dashboard for monitoring all LangServe deployments.

- Reduces debugging time by offering detailed insights into workflow performance.

- Enhances user experience by quickly identifying and resolving issues.

LangSmith integrates seamlessly with LangServe, offering native support for tracing and monitoring without additional setup.

6.2 Setting Up Tracing and Logging

LangServe provides built-in support for tracing and logging, enabling you to monitor application activity and debug issues effectively.

Step 1: Enable Tracing in LangServe

Tracing allows you to follow the flow of each request within the LangChain application.

Example Configuration: Add tracing support to your LangChain application:

python

```
from langchain import PromptTemplate, LLMChain
from langserve import serve


# Import LangSmith for tracing
```

```python
from langsmith.tracer import enable_tracing


# Define the workflow
prompt = PromptTemplate(
    input_variables=["name"],
    template="Hello {name}, how can I assist you today?"
)
chain = LLMChain(prompt_template=prompt,
llm="openai-gpt3")


# Enable tracing
enable_tracing()


# Serve the application
if __name__ == "__main__":
    serve(chain)
```

Step 2: Configure Logging

Logging captures application activity and errors in real-time.

Enable Debug-Level Logging:

bash

```bash
python app.py --log-level debug
```

Output Example:

css

[DEBUG] Received request at /invoke

[INFO] Workflow started for input: {"name": "Alice"}

[INFO] Workflow completed with output: {"response": "Hello Alice, how can I assist you today?"}

Step 3: Set Up Log Files

Redirect logs to a file for later analysis:

bash

```
python app.py --log-level debug > app_logs.log
2>&1
```

6.3 Monitoring Application Health and Performance Metrics

Effective monitoring ensures that your LangServe application meets user demands and operates reliably.

Key Metrics to Monitor:

1. **Latency**:

   o Measures the time taken to process a request.

   o High latency indicates potential bottlenecks.

2. **Throughput**:

- o The number of requests processed per second.

- o Critical for high-traffic applications.

3. **Error Rates**:

- o Tracks the percentage of failed requests.

- o Helps identify recurring issues.

4. **Resource Usage**:

- o Monitors CPU, memory, and disk usage.

- o Ensures the server is not overloaded.

Monitoring Tools:

1. **LangSmith Dashboard**:

- o Displays real-time metrics and traces.

- o Offers visualizations for latency and throughput trends.

2. **Third-Party Tools**:

- o Integrate LangServe with tools like **Prometheus** or **Grafana** for advanced monitoring.

Example Dashboard Metrics:

Metric	Current Value	Threshold	Status
Latency (ms)	120	<200	☐ Healthy
Throughput (req/s)	50	>40	☐ Healthy

Metric	Current Value	Threshold	Status
Error Rate (%)	1.2	<5	☐ Healthy
CPU Usage (%)	70	<85	☐ Healthy

6.4 Troubleshooting with LangSmith

LangSmith provides powerful tools for troubleshooting issues in LangServe applications.

Step 1: Analyze Traces

Use LangSmith's trace viewer to:

- Identify bottlenecks in workflows.

- Trace specific requests to pinpoint errors.

Example Workflow Trace:

css

```
1. Received input: {"name": "Alice"}

2. Prompt executed: "Hello Alice, how can I
assist you today?"

3. Response generated: {"response": "Hello Alice,
how can I assist you today?"}
```

4. Sent response back to client.

Step 2: Inspect Error Logs

Review logs for error messages or warnings. Example:

css

```
[ERROR] Invalid input schema: {"age": 25} does
not match expected schema: {"name": "string"}
```

Solution: Ensure the client sends valid input matching the schema.

Step 3: Monitor Latency Trends

Check latency spikes to identify slow-performing workflows. Example:

- If latency increases during specific times, the server may need more workers or load balancing.

6.5 Example: Debugging a Slow-Performing API

This example demonstrates how to debug and optimize a slow-performing LangServe application.

Problem:

A chatbot API has high latency, taking 2-3 seconds to respond.

Step 1: Enable Tracing

Add tracing to the application:

python

```
from langsmith.tracer import enable_tracing
# Enable tracing
enable_tracing()
```

Step 2: Collect Performance Data

Run the application and analyze traces in LangSmith.

Trace Example:

vbnet

Step 1: Input received (0ms)

Step 2: LLM request sent to OpenAI (1000ms)

Step 3: LLM response received (1500ms)

Step 4: Output processed (2000ms)

Observation:

- The delay is caused by the LLM response time.

Step 3: Optimize LLM Requests

Reduce latency by:

1. **Switching to a Faster Model**:

   o Replace openai-gpt3 with a smaller, faster model.

   o Example:

python

llm="openai-gpt3-turbo"

2. **Caching Responses**:

   o   Use caching to store frequent responses.

   o   Example:

python

```
from cachetools import cached, TTLCache
cache = TTLCache(maxsize=100, ttl=300)
@cached(cache)
def get_response(input_data):
    return chain.run(input_data)
```

Step 4: Test Optimization

Re-test the API and observe improvements in latency.

Before Optimization:

Request	Latency (ms)
1	2200
2	2100

After Optimization:

Request	Latency (ms)
1	800
2	850

By leveraging LangSmith for monitoring and troubleshooting, you can ensure your LangServe applications are reliable, efficient, and ready to handle production workloads. This chapter equips you with the tools and techniques to diagnose and resolve performance issues effectively.

Chapter 7: Security and Authentication

7.1 Securing Your LangServe APIs: Best Practices

APIs deployed using LangServe may handle sensitive data or be exposed to high traffic, making security essential. This section outlines best practices to ensure your APIs remain protected and reliable.

1. Use HTTPS

- Always use HTTPS to encrypt data transmitted between clients and your API server.

- Benefits:

    o Prevents data interception (man-in-the-middle attacks).

    o Builds trust with users by showing secure connections.

- Implementation:

    o Use tools like NGINX or AWS Elastic Load Balancer to enable HTTPS.

2. Require Authentication

- Ensure that only authorized users can access your APIs.

- Common methods:

- API Key Authentication: Simple and widely supported.

- OAuth2: For advanced scenarios with third-party authentication providers.

3. Validate Input Data

- Prevent malicious inputs by validating all incoming requests.

- Example:

python

```python
import re

def validate_input(data):
    if not isinstance(data.get("name"), str) or not re.match(r"^[a-zA-Z]+$", data["name"]):
        raise ValueError("Invalid input format")
```

4. Implement Rate Limiting

- Limit the number of requests a client can send in a specific time frame.

- Benefits:

  - Protects against DDoS attacks.

  - Prevents abuse by malicious users.

5. Log and Monitor Activity

- Record API requests and responses to detect unauthorized access or suspicious behavior.

- Use monitoring tools like LangSmith to visualize API usage.

6. Regularly Update Dependencies

- Keep LangServe, LangChain, and all related libraries up to date to protect against known vulnerabilities.

7. Secure Server Configuration

- Disable unnecessary ports and services.

- Use firewalls to block unauthorized access.

7.2 Implementing API Key Authentication

API key authentication is a straightforward method to control access to your LangServe APIs.

What Is an API Key?

An API key is a unique identifier used to authenticate clients accessing your API. It's included in requests as a header or query parameter.

How API Keys Work

1. The server generates and shares a unique API key with each authorized client.

2. Clients include the API key in their requests.

3. The server verifies the key before processing the request.

Implementation Steps

Step 1: Generate an API Key Generate a random API key:

python

```
import secrets

api_key = secrets.token_hex(32)

print(f"Generated API Key: {api_key}")
```

Step 2: Securely Store the API Key

- Store API keys in environment variables or secure storage.

- Example .env file:

text

API_KEY=your_generated_api_key

Step 3: Validate API Keys in LangServe Modify your LangServe application to check for a valid API key:

python

```
import os

from fastapi import Request, HTTPException

from langchain import PromptTemplate, LLMChain

from langserve import serve


# Load API key from environment

API_KEY = os.getenv("API_KEY")
```

```python
# Middleware for API key validation
async def validate_api_key(request: Request):
    key = request.headers.get("x-api-key")
    if key != API_KEY:
        raise HTTPException(status_code=401,
detail="Unauthorized")


# Define the LangChain application
prompt = PromptTemplate(input_variables=["name"],
template="Hello {name}, welcome to LangServe!")
chain = LLMChain(prompt_template=prompt,
llm="openai-gpt3")


# Serve the application with API key validation
if __name__ == "__main__":
    serve(chain, middleware=[validate_api_key])
```

Step 4: Test API Key Authentication

- Send a request with the API key:

bash

```bash
curl -X POST http://localhost:8000/invoke \
    -H "x-api-key: your_generated_api_key" \
    -H "Content-Type: application/json" \
    -d '{"name": "Alice"}'
```

Expected Response:

json

```json
{
  "response": "Hello Alice, welcome to LangServe!"
}
```

- Send a request without the API key:

bash

```bash
curl -X POST http://localhost:8000/invoke \
    -H "Content-Type: application/json" \
    -d '{"name": "Alice"}'
```

Expected Response:

json

```json
{
  "detail": "Unauthorized"
}
```

7.3 Rate Limiting and Throttling

Rate limiting controls the number of requests a client can send in a specific time frame, preventing overuse or abuse.

Benefits of Rate Limiting

1. Protects against denial-of-service (DoS) attacks.

2. Ensures fair usage among clients.

3. Reduces server overload during traffic spikes.

Implementation in LangServe

Step 1: Install a Rate Limiting Library Use a library like slowapi for rate limiting:

bash

```
pip install slowapi
```

Step 2: Configure Rate Limiting Integrate rate limiting into your LangServe application:

python

```
from slowapi import Limiter

from slowapi.util import import get_remote_address

from fastapi import FastAPI, Request,
HTTPException

from langchain import PromptTemplate, LLMChain

from langserve import serve


# Initialize the rate limiter

limiter = Limiter(key_func=get_remote_address)


# Define the LangChain application

prompt = PromptTemplate(input_variables=["name"],
template="Hello {name}, welcome to LangServe!")
```

```python
chain = LLMChain(prompt_template=prompt,
llm="openai-gpt3")


# Apply rate limiting middleware

@limiter.limit("10/minute")

async def rate_limited_endpoint(request:
Request):

    pass


# Serve the application with rate limiting

if __name__ == "__main__":

    serve(chain,
middleware=[rate_limited_endpoint])
```

Step 3: Test Rate Limiting Send more than 10 requests within a minute:

bash

```bash
curl -X POST http://localhost:8000/invoke \

    -H "x-api-key: your_generated_api_key" \

    -H "Content-Type: application/json" \

    -d '{"name": "Alice"}'
```

- After exceeding the limit, you'll receive:

json

```json
{

  "detail": "Too Many Requests"
```

```
}
```

7.4 Example: Adding Authentication to a Deployed API

This example demonstrates combining API key authentication and rate limiting for a secure LangServe API.

Step 1: Define the Application

Create a chatbot application with authentication and rate limiting:

python

```python
import os

from slowapi import Limiter

from slowapi.util import get_remote_address

from fastapi import Request, HTTPException

from langchain import PromptTemplate, LLMChain

from langserve import serve


# Load API key

API_KEY = os.getenv("API_KEY")


# Initialize rate limiter

limiter = Limiter(key_func=get_remote_address)


# Middleware for API key validation
```

```python
async def validate_api_key(request: Request):

    key = request.headers.get("x-api-key")

    if key != API_KEY:

        raise HTTPException(status_code=401,
detail="Unauthorized")


# Define LangChain application

prompt = PromptTemplate(input_variables=["name"],
template="Hello {name}, welcome to our secure
service!")

chain = LLMChain(prompt_template=prompt,
llm="openai-gpt3")


# Apply middleware

middleware = [validate_api_key,
limiter.limit("5/minute")]


# Serve the application

if __name__ == "__main__":

    serve(chain, middleware=middleware)
```

Step 2: Deploy and Test

1. Deploy the application:

bash

python secure_chatbot.py

2. Test with a valid API key:

bash

```bash
curl -X POST http://localhost:8000/invoke \
    -H "x-api-key: your_generated_api_key" \
    -H "Content-Type: application/json" \
    -d '{"name": "Bob"}'
```

Response:

json

```json
{
    "response": "Hello Bob, welcome to our secure
service!"
}
```

Exceed the rate limit and observe the error response:

json

```json
{
    "detail": "Too Many Requests"
}
```

By implementing API key authentication, rate limiting, and adhering to security best practices, you can protect your LangServe APIs against unauthorized access, abuse, and performance degradation. These strategies ensure your APIs remain secure, reliable, and ready for production use.

Chapter 8: Advanced Configuration and Customization

8.1 Customizing LangServe Settings for Specific Use Cases

LangServe provides a flexible configuration system that allows you to customize its behavior to meet the specific needs of your application. Whether optimizing performance, enabling advanced features, or managing unique workflows, customizing LangServe settings can help you achieve your goals.

Common Customization Scenarios

1. **Port Configuration**:

   o Customize the port number to avoid conflicts with other applications.

   o Example:

bash

```
python app.py --port 8080
```

2. **Worker Settings**:

   o Adjust the number of workers to optimize resource usage and handle traffic efficiently.

   o Example:

bash

```
python app.py --workers 4
```

3. **Timeout Configuration**:

   o Define request timeouts to terminate unresponsive workflows gracefully.

   o Example:

bash

```
python app.py --timeout 30
```

4. **Logging Levels**:

   o Customize the verbosity of logs for debugging or monitoring purposes.

   o Options: debug, info, warning, error

   o Example:

bash

```
python app.py --log-level debug
```

5. **Middleware**:

   o Add custom middleware for pre- or post-processing of requests.

   o Example:

python

```
async def custom_middleware(request, next_call):
    print("Custom Middleware: Request Received")
    response = await next_call(request)
    print("Custom Middleware: Response Sent")
    return response
serve(chain, middleware=[custom_middleware])
```

Customization Best Practices

- Document all changes to your configuration for maintainability.

- Test configurations in a staging environment before deploying to production.

- Monitor performance to ensure that custom settings do not introduce bottlenecks.

8.2 Using Environment Variables for Dynamic Configuration

Environment variables are a secure and efficient way to manage configuration settings. They allow you to separate configuration from code, making your application more flexible and secure.

Why Use Environment Variables?

- **Security**: Protect sensitive information such as API keys and database credentials.

- **Flexibility**: Change configuration settings without modifying the codebase.

- **Portability**: Use the same code across multiple environments (e.g., development, staging, production).

Setting Environment Variables

1. **Create a .env File**:

   o Example:

text

API_KEY=your_api_key

PORT=8000

WORKERS=4

2. **Load Variables in Python**:

   o Use the dotenv package to load environment variables.

   o Installation:

bash

```bash
pip install python-dotenv
```

   o Example Code:

python

```python
import os

from dotenv import load_dotenv

from langchain import PromptTemplate, LLMChain

from langserve import serve
```

```python
# Load environment variables
load_dotenv()

# Access variables
api_key = os.getenv("API_KEY")
port = int(os.getenv("PORT", 8000))
workers = int(os.getenv("WORKERS", 1))

# Define a LangChain application
prompt = PromptTemplate(
    input_variables=["name"],
    template="Hello {name}, your API key is {api_key}."
)
chain = LLMChain(prompt_template=prompt, llm="openai-gpt3")

# Serve the application
if __name__ == "__main__":
    serve(chain, port=port, workers=workers)
```

Example Use Cases

1. Securely storing API keys:

text

OPENAI_API_KEY=your_openai_api_key

2. Configuring different environments:

text

```
# Development

DEBUG=true


# Production

DEBUG=false
```

8.3 Advanced Use of the LangServe Playground

The LangServe Playground is a user-friendly interface that allows developers to experiment with configurations, test inputs, and observe outputs without writing additional code. It is an invaluable tool for debugging and prototyping.

Key Features of the Playground

1. **Interactive Input Testing**:

   o Enter sample inputs directly in the UI and observe the outputs.

2. **Schema Visualization**:

   o View the input/output schema of your LangChain application.

3. **Real-Time Debugging**:

   o   Inspect request logs and execution traces for each invocation.

Accessing the Playground

- By default, the LangServe Playground is available at /playground.

- Example:

   o   Start LangServe:

bash

```
python app.py
```

   o   Access the playground at http://localhost:8000/playground.

Advanced Configurations in the Playground

1. **Test with Batch Inputs**:

   o   Upload a JSON file with multiple inputs and observe batch processing results.

2. **Custom Endpoint Testing**:

   o   Experiment with /invoke, /batch, and /stream endpoints using the UI.

3. **Tuning Parameters**:

   o   Dynamically adjust parameters such as temperature or response length for LLM workflows.

8.4 Example: Configuring LangServe for Streaming Outputs

Streaming outputs allow LangServe to send partial responses incrementally, reducing wait times for clients. This feature is ideal for real-time applications such as chatbots or live data analysis.

Step 1: Define a Streaming Workflow

Modify your LangChain application to support streaming:

python

```python
from langchain import PromptTemplate, LLMChain

from langserve import serve


# Define a prompt template

prompt = PromptTemplate(

    input_variables=["query"],

    template="Processing your query:
{query}\nPartial response follows..."

)


# Create a LangChain workflow

chain = LLMChain(prompt_template=prompt,
llm="openai-gpt3")


# Enable streaming mode
```

```python
if __name__ == "__main__":
    serve(chain, streaming=True)
```

Step 2: Test the Streaming API

- Start the server:

bash

```bash
python app.py
```

- Send a streaming request using curl:

bash

curl -X POST http://localhost:8000/stream \

   -H "Content-Type: application/json" \

   -d '{"query": "Explain quantum physics"}'

Expected Output:

python

```
Processing your query: Explain quantum physics
Partial response follows...
Quantum
physics
is
the
study
of
```

. . .

Step 3: Integrate Streaming in Client Applications

Use WebSockets or HTTP/2 to handle streaming responses in your frontend.

This chapter explored advanced configuration and customization options in LangServe, empowering you to adapt the platform for specific use cases. By leveraging environment variables, the LangServe Playground, and streaming outputs, you can enhance the functionality, security, and usability of your LangServe applications. These skills prepare you to handle complex deployment scenarios with confidence.

Chapter 9: Real-World Applications of LangServe

LangServe opens up possibilities for building and deploying scalable, production-ready AI applications. This chapter explores practical, real-world use cases, showcasing how LangServe can be leveraged to create chatbots, knowledge retrieval systems, real-time data processing APIs, and solutions for various industries.

9.1 Chatbots and Conversational Agents

Overview

Chatbots and conversational agents use natural language processing (NLP) to engage users in text or voice-based interactions. LangServe makes it easy to deploy LangChain-based chatbots as scalable APIs.

Applications

1. **Customer Support**:

   o Responding to frequently asked questions.

   o Automating ticket routing and resolution.

2. **Virtual Assistants**:

   o Scheduling appointments.

   o Providing personalized recommendations.

Example: Deploying a Customer Support Chatbot

Step 1: Define the Chatbot Workflow

python

```python
from langchain import PromptTemplate, LLMChain
from langserve import serve


# Define the prompt template
prompt = PromptTemplate(
    input_variables=["query"],
    template="User: {query}\nBot: I'm here to
assist you. Let me find an answer!"
)


# Create the chatbot workflow
chain = LLMChain(prompt_template=prompt,
llm="openai-gpt3")


# Serve the chatbot
if __name__ == "__main__":
    serve(chain)
```

Step 2: Test the Chatbot API Use curl to test the chatbot:

bash

```
curl -X POST http://localhost:8000/invoke \
     -H "Content-Type: application/json" \
     -d '{"query": "What is the return policy?"}'
```

Response:

json

```
{
    "response": "User: What is the return
policy?\nBot: I'm here to assist you. Let me find
an answer!"
}
```

9.2 Knowledge Retrieval Systems

Overview

Knowledge retrieval systems enable efficient querying of large datasets, such as documents, research papers, or FAQs. LangServe can deploy these systems to serve as APIs that answer user queries by retrieving relevant information.

Applications

1. **Corporate Intranets**:

   o Employees search for internal policies or documents.

2. **Educational Platforms**:

   o Students query databases of research materials.

3. **Customer Portals**:

   o   Users find answers in extensive knowledge bases.

Example: Deploying a Document Search API

Step 1: Define the Workflow

python

```
from langchain.document_loaders import TextLoader

from langchain.vectorstores import FAISS

from langchain.embeddings import OpenAIEmbeddings

from langchain.chains import RetrievalQA

from langserve import serve


# Load documents

loader = TextLoader("company_policies.txt")

documents = loader.load()


# Build a vector store

vectorstore = FAISS.from_documents(documents,
OpenAIEmbeddings())


# Create a Retrieval-based QA chain

retrieval_qa =
RetrievalQA(vectorstore.as_retriever())
```

```
# Serve the knowledge retrieval system

if __name__ == "__main__":

    serve(retrieval_qa)
```

Step 2: Test the API

bash

```
curl -X POST http://localhost:8000/invoke \

     -H "Content-Type: application/json" \

     -d '{"query": "What is the company holiday
policy?"}'
```

Response:

json

```
{

    "response": "The company holiday policy
states that employees are entitled to 10 paid
holidays annually."

}
```

9.3 Real-Time Data Processing APIs

Overview

Real-time data processing APIs handle incoming streams of data and provide immediate insights or outputs. LangServe's streaming capabilities are ideal for these applications.

Applications

1. **Sentiment Analysis**:

    o Analyze social media posts in real time.

2. **Financial Markets**:

    o Process stock price data to generate alerts.

3. **IoT Systems**:

    o Analyze sensor data for predictive maintenance.

Example: Deploying a Sentiment Analysis API

Step 1: Define the Sentiment Analysis Workflow

python

```python
from langchain import PromptTemplate, LLMChain
from langserve import serve


# Define the sentiment analysis prompt
prompt = PromptTemplate(
    input_variables=["text"],
    template="Analyze the sentiment of the
following text: {text}"
)


# Create the sentiment analysis workflow
```

```
chain = LLMChain(prompt_template=prompt,
llm="openai-gpt3")


# Serve the workflow
if __name__ == "__main__":
    serve(chain, streaming=True)
```

Step 2: Test the Streaming API

bash

```
curl -X POST http://localhost:8000/stream \
     -H "Content-Type: application/json" \
     -d '{"text": "I love this product!"}'
```

Response:

arduino

Analyze

the

sentiment

of

the

following

text:

Positive.

9.4 Industry Use Cases: Customer Support, Healthcare, E-commerce

Customer Support

LangServe enables automation in customer support systems, helping businesses reduce response times and improve customer satisfaction.

Example: Automated Ticketing System

- Workflow: Analyze customer queries and route tickets to the appropriate department.

- LangServe Benefit: Scalability to handle thousands of queries simultaneously.

Healthcare

AI in healthcare streamlines patient support, diagnosis, and knowledge retrieval.

Example: Medical Knowledge Retrieval

- Workflow: Answer doctors' questions using a database of research papers.

- LangServe Benefit: Quick, accurate retrieval of relevant medical information.

E-commerce

AI applications in e-commerce enhance customer experience and increase sales.

Example: Personalized Product Recommendations

- Workflow: Use user behavior data to recommend products.

- LangServe Benefit: Real-time deployment of recommendation algorithms.

This chapter demonstrates the versatility of LangServe across various real-world applications, from chatbots to knowledge retrieval systems, real-time data processing APIs, and industry-specific solutions. By understanding these use cases, developers can leverage LangServe to create impactful, scalable AI-powered systems for diverse domains.

Chapter 10: Building a Chatbot API with LangServe

Chatbots have become a cornerstone of AI applications, offering instant, automated assistance in customer support, e-commerce, education, and more. In this chapter, we will build a chatbot API step-by-step using LangChain and LangServe, covering design principles, workflow preparation, deployment, and testing. By the end of the chapter, you'll also see an example of a fully functional customer support chatbot.

10.1 Designing the Chatbot

Before diving into implementation, designing the chatbot is critical to ensure it meets user needs effectively.

Define the Purpose

- Identify the chatbot's main goal.

    - Example: A customer support chatbot designed to answer common queries like return policies, product details, and order tracking.

Understand User Requirements

- Typical user needs for a customer support chatbot:

    1. Quick and accurate responses to FAQs.

    2. Escalation to human support if the chatbot cannot resolve the query.

Choose the Interaction Style

- Decide how the chatbot will communicate:

    o Formal: Suitable for corporate or healthcare use cases.

    o Casual: Ideal for e-commerce and entertainment platforms.

Define Inputs and Outputs

Input	Example
User's query text	"What is the return policy?"
Context (optional)	Order ID, customer name

Output	Example
Bot's response text	"You can return items within 30 days."

10.2 Preparing LangChain Workflows

LangChain workflows define the chatbot's functionality, including prompt templates, memory, and additional tools like databases or APIs.

Step 1: Define the Prompt Template

A prompt template determines how user input is processed. For a customer support chatbot:

python

```python
from langchain import PromptTemplate


prompt = PromptTemplate(

    input_variables=["query"],

    template="You are a helpful customer support
bot. Respond professionally to the following
query: {query}"

)
```

Step 2: Add Tools (Optional)

If the chatbot requires additional capabilities like retrieving product details from a database, integrate relevant tools:

python

```python
from langchain.tools import Tool

product_tool = Tool(

    name="product_info",

    func=lambda product_id: f"Details for product
{product_id}.",

    description="Provides information about
products."

)
```

Step 3: Create the LangChain Workflow

Combine the prompt and tools into a LangChain workflow:

python

```python
from langchain import LLMChain

llm_chain = LLMChain(prompt_template=prompt,
llm="openai-gpt3")
```

10.3 Deploying with LangServe

LangServe simplifies deployment by wrapping the LangChain workflow into a RESTful API.

Step 1: Install LangServe

Ensure LangServe is installed in your environment:

bash

```bash
pip install langserve
```

Step 2: Create the LangServe Application

Save the following code in a file named chatbot.py:

python

```python
from langchain import PromptTemplate, LLMChain
from langserve import serve


# Define the prompt
prompt = PromptTemplate(

    input_variables=["query"],

    template="You are a professional customer
support bot. Respond to: {query}"
```

```
)


# Create the LangChain workflow

llm_chain = LLMChain(prompt_template=prompt,
llm="openai-gpt3")


# Deploy with LangServe

if __name__ == "__main__":

    serve(llm_chain)
```

Step 3: Run the LangServe Server

Start the server:

bash

```
python chatbot.py
```
```
The server will run at http://localhost:8000.
```

10.4 Testing the Chatbot API with Postman

Step 1: Open Postman

Download and install Postman from Postman's official site.

Step 2: Create a New Request

1. Select **POST** as the request method.

2. Enter the API endpoint:

bash

```
http://localhost:8000/invoke
```

Step 3: Configure the Headers

Add a header to specify the content type:

Key	Value
Content-Type	application/json

Step 4: Provide the Request Body

Send the user's query as JSON in the request body:

json

```json
{
  "query": "What is the return policy?"
}
```

Step 5: Send the Request

Click **Send** to invoke the chatbot API.

Step 6: Analyze the Response

The expected response:

json

```json
{
  "response": "You can return items within 30 days."
}
```

10.5 Example: A Customer Support Chatbot

This example builds a fully functional customer support chatbot capable of answering queries and escalating to a human agent when necessary.

Step 1: Define the Chatbot Workflow

Create the chatbot with escalation logic:

python

```python
from langchain import PromptTemplate, LLMChain

from langserve import serve


# Define the prompt with escalation

prompt = PromptTemplate(

    input_variables=["query"],

    template=(

        "You are a customer support chatbot. If
you cannot answer, escalate to a human."

        "\nUser query: {query}\nResponse:"

    )

)


# Create the LangChain workflow

llm_chain = LLMChain(prompt_template=prompt,
llm="openai-gpt3")
```

```
# Serve the chatbot API

if __name__ == "__main__":

    serve(llm_chain)
```

Step 2: Add Escalation Logic

Update the chatbot to include escalation:

python

```python
def escalate_to_human(query):

    return "I'm unable to assist with this query.
Escalating to a human agent."


llm_chain = LLMChain(

    prompt_template=prompt,

    llm="openai-gpt3",

    post_process_func=lambda response: response
if "escalate" not in response.lower() else
escalate_to_human(response)

)
```

Step 3: Deploy and Test

1. Run the server:

bash

```bash
python chatbot.py
```

2. Test with queries:

- Query: "What is the return policy?" Response: "You can return items within 30 days."

- Query: "Can I change my account email?" Response: "I'm unable to assist with this query. Escalating to a human agent."

This chapter provided a detailed walkthrough of building, deploying, and testing a chatbot API using LangServe. You learned how to design the chatbot, prepare LangChain workflows, and implement advanced features like escalation. With these skills, you can develop robust chatbot solutions for diverse use cases, including customer support, virtual assistants, and more.

Chapter 11: Knowledge Retrieval System with LangServe

Knowledge retrieval systems are integral to businesses, enabling users to efficiently search and retrieve relevant information from large datasets. This chapter will guide you through setting up a knowledge retrieval system using LangChain, deploying it with LangServe, fine-tuning for accuracy, and implementing a practical example for a corporate intranet.

11.1 Setting up a Knowledge Base with LangChain

A knowledge base is the foundation of any retrieval system. It contains structured or unstructured data indexed for efficient querying.

Step 1: Prepare Your Data

1. **Identify Relevant Documents**:

   o Collect documents such as PDFs, text files, or web pages.

   o Example: Company policies, technical manuals, and FAQs.

2. **Format Your Data**:

   o Convert all documents into plain text for processing.

   o Example using Python:

python

```python
import os

def load_text_files(directory):

    documents = []

    for filename in os.listdir(directory):

        with open(os.path.join(directory,
filename), 'r') as file:

            documents.append(file.read())

    return documents
```

Step 2: Create a Knowledge Base

Use LangChain to create a knowledge base using embeddings for efficient search and retrieval.

python

```python
from langchain.document_loaders import TextLoader

from langchain.vectorstores import FAISS

from langchain.embeddings import OpenAIEmbeddings


# Load documents from text files

loader = TextLoader("./data")

documents = loader.load()


# Create embeddings and vector store

vectorstore = FAISS.from_documents(documents,
OpenAIEmbeddings())
```

Step 3: Save the Vector Store

Save the vector store for use in the retrieval system:

python

```
vectorstore.save_local("./vectorstore")
```

11.2 Deploying a Search and Retrieval API

Deploy the knowledge retrieval system with LangServe to provide a scalable, API-based interface for querying the knowledge base.

Step 1: Load the Vector Store

Ensure the vector store is loaded correctly in your API application:

python

```
from langchain.vectorstores import FAISS
from langchain.chains import import RetrievalQA
from langserve import serve


# Load the vector store
vectorstore = FAISS.load_local("./vectorstore")


# Create a retrieval-based QA system
retriever = vectorstore.as_retriever()
qa_chain = RetrievalQA(retriever=retriever)
```

Step 2: Deploy the API

Wrap the retrieval workflow with LangServe:

python

```python
if __name__ == "__main__":
    serve(qa_chain)
```

Step 3: Start the Server

Run the application:

bash

```bash
python retrieval_api.py
```

The API is now live at http://localhost:8000.

Step 4: Test the Retrieval API

Use curl to test:

bash

```bash
curl -X POST http://localhost:8000/invoke \
    -H "Content-Type: application/json" \
    -d '{"query": "What is the company holiday policy?"}'
```

Response:

json

```json
{
    "response": "The company holiday policy states that employees are entitled to 10 paid holidays annually."
}
```

11.3 Fine-Tuning for Relevance and Accuracy

Fine-tuning ensures that your knowledge retrieval system delivers accurate and relevant responses.

1. Optimize Document Embeddings

- Use domain-specific embeddings if available (e.g., for legal or medical data).

- Example:

python

```
from langchain.embeddings import
HuggingFaceEmbeddings


embeddings =
HuggingFaceEmbeddings(model_name="sentence-
transformers/all-MiniLM-L6-v2")

vectorstore = FAISS.from_documents(documents,
embeddings)
```

2. Enhance Retrieval Strategies

- Experiment with different retrieval methods:

  - **Similarity Search**: Returns results based on vector similarity.

  - **Hybrid Search**: Combines keyword and vector-based search.

- Example for hybrid search:

python

```
retriever =
vectorstore.as_retriever(search_type="mmr",
search_kwargs={"k": 5})
```

3. Use Feedback Loops

- Collect feedback on API responses and refine the system.

- Example:

  o Track user satisfaction with responses using
    metadata.

  o Adjust weights or embeddings based on feedback.

4. Test and Validate

- Regularly test the system with benchmark queries to ensure
  relevance.

- Automate testing:

python

```
test_queries = ["What is the holiday policy?",
"How do I reset my password?"]

for query in test_queries:

    print(qa_chain.run({"query": query}))
```

11.4 Example: Document Search for a Corporate Intranet

This example demonstrates a practical application of a knowledge
retrieval system for a corporate intranet.

Objective

Allow employees to query company policies and technical documentation through an API.

Step 1: Prepare the Data

Store corporate documents in the ./data directory:

- holiday_policy.txt

- technical_manual.txt

Step 2: Create the Retrieval Workflow

python

```python
from langchain.document_loaders import TextLoader

from langchain.vectorstores import FAISS

from langchain.embeddings import OpenAIEmbeddings

from langchain.chains import RetrievalQA

from langserve import serve


# Load and process documents

loader = TextLoader("./data")

documents = loader.load()

vectorstore = FAISS.from_documents(documents,
OpenAIEmbeddings())


# Build the retrieval system

retriever = vectorstore.as_retriever()
```

```
qa_chain = RetrievalQA(retriever=retriever)


# Deploy the API
if __name__ == "__main__":
    serve(qa_chain)
```

Step 3: Deploy the API

Run the application:

bash

```
python intranet_api.py
```

Step 4: Test the API

Query the knowledge base:

bash

```
curl -X POST http://localhost:8000/invoke \
    -H "Content-Type: application/json" \
    -d '{"query": "How do I file an expense report?"}'
```

Response:

json

```
{
    "response": "To file an expense report,
complete the online form available on the
intranet under 'Finance'."
}
```

In this chapter, you've learned how to build and deploy a knowledge retrieval system using LangChain and LangServe. By setting up a knowledge base, deploying a retrieval API, and fine-tuning for accuracy, you can create efficient systems for real-world applications like corporate intranets, customer portals, and educational platforms. The provided example highlights how such systems can simplify access to information and improve organizational efficiency.

Chapter 12: Real-Time Streaming API with LangServe

Real-time streaming APIs allow applications to process and send data incrementally as it is generated, providing faster response times and reducing latency. In this chapter, we will explore streaming capabilities in LangServe, deploy a real-time sentiment analysis application, configure LangServe for streaming outputs, and demonstrate a practical example using live social media data.

12.1 Understanding Streaming in LangServe

What Is Streaming?

Streaming is a method of transmitting data incrementally rather than waiting for the entire result to be ready. In LangServe, streaming enables:

1. **Faster Responses**:

   o Partial results are sent to the client as soon as they are available.

2. **Reduced Memory Usage**:

   o Data is processed in chunks, minimizing resource demands.

3. **Improved User Experience**:

   o Real-time feedback enhances interactive applications like chatbots or dashboards.

Benefits of Streaming in LangServe

- **Real-Time Interactions**: Ideal for applications like sentiment analysis, live transcription, and chatbots.

- **Efficiency**: Reduces wait times for large responses.

- **Scalability**: Handles high traffic by breaking responses into smaller segments.

How LangServe Handles Streaming

LangServe integrates seamlessly with LangChain workflows to stream outputs:

- Streaming is enabled by setting streaming=True when deploying the LangChain workflow.

- The /stream endpoint processes requests and streams results.

12.2 Deploying a Real-Time Sentiment Analysis Application

Objective

Deploy an API that analyzes sentiment in real-time, returning a stream of tokens representing the sentiment analysis output.

Step 1: Define the Sentiment Analysis Workflow

python

```python
from langchain import PromptTemplate, LLMChain
from langserve import serve


# Define the prompt template
prompt = PromptTemplate(
    input_variables=["text"],
    template="Analyze the sentiment of the
following text: {text}\nPartial response
follows..."
)


# Create a sentiment analysis workflow
chain = LLMChain(prompt_template=prompt,
llm="openai-gpt3")


# Enable streaming
if __name__ == "__main__":
    serve(chain, streaming=True)
```

Step 2: Save and Run the Application

Save the script as sentiment_analysis.py and start the LangServe server:

bash

```
python sentiment_analysis.py
```

Step 3: Test the Streaming API

Use curl to send a request:

bash

```
curl -X POST http://localhost:8000/stream \

    -H "Content-Type: application/json" \

    -d '{"text": "I love this product. It is amazing!"}'
```

Expected Output (streamed):

arduino

Analyze

the

sentiment

of

the

following

text:

Positive.

12.3 Configuring LangServe for Streaming Outputs

Step 1: Enable Streaming in LangServe

When deploying the LangChain workflow, set the streaming=True parameter:

python

```python
serve(chain, streaming=True)
```

Step 2: Adjust Server Configuration

Optimize the server for streaming:

1. **Increase Worker Count**:

   o Ensure sufficient workers to handle concurrent streaming requests:

bash

```bash
python sentiment_analysis.py --workers 4
```

2. **Adjust Timeout Settings**:

   o Set appropriate timeouts for long-running streaming requests:

bash

```bash
python sentiment_analysis.py --timeout 60
```

Step 3: Handle Partial Results

Streaming APIs send partial results as chunks. Ensure the client application can handle incremental responses, such as:

- Displaying tokens as they arrive (e.g., in a chatbot UI).

- Aggregating results for final processing.

12.4 Example: Processing Live Social Media Data

Objective

Create a real-time streaming API to analyze the sentiment of live social media data, such as tweets.

Step 1: Integrate a Social Media API

Use a library like tweepy to stream live tweets:

bash

```
pip install tweepy
```

Step 2: Define the Workflow

Create a script to fetch tweets and process them using LangServe.

Fetch Tweets:

python

```
import tweepy
# Twitter API credentials
api_key = "your_api_key"
api_secret = "your_api_secret"
access_token = "your_access_token"
access_token_secret = "your_access_token_secret"
```

```python
# Authenticate with Twitter API

auth = tweepy.OAuth1UserHandler(api_key,
api_secret, access_token, access_token_secret)

api = tweepy.API(auth)


# Stream tweets with specific keywords

class MyStreamListener(tweepy.StreamListener):

    def on_status(self, status):

        print(status.text)


stream_listener = MyStreamListener()

stream = tweepy.Stream(auth=api.auth,
listener=stream_listener)

stream.filter(track=["product", "review"],
languages=["en"])
```

Integrate LangServe Sentiment Analysis:

python

```python
import requests

# LangServe API endpoint

url = "http://localhost:8000/stream"


class MyStreamListener(tweepy.StreamListener):

    def on_status(self, status):

        # Send tweet text to LangServe for
sentiment analysis
```

```python
        response = requests.post(url,
json={"text": status.text}, stream=True)
        for chunk in
response.iter_content(chunk_size=1024):
            print(chunk.decode("utf-8"))


stream_listener = MyStreamListener()

stream = tweepy.Stream(auth=api.auth,
listener=stream_listener)

stream.filter(track=["product", "review"],
languages=["en"])
```

Step 3: Test the Workflow

Run the script to start processing live tweets:

bash

```
python live_sentiment_analysis.py
```

Expected Output (streamed):

vbnet

```
Tweet: "This product is amazing!"

Sentiment: Positive.

Tweet: "I'm disappointed with this purchase."

Sentiment: Negative.
```

In this chapter, you've learned how to implement real-time streaming APIs using LangServe, focusing on a sentiment analysis application. The example of processing live social media data highlights the power of LangServe for real-time tasks. By leveraging these skills, you can create interactive, efficient APIs for use cases like live analytics, chatbot responses, and more.

Chapter 13: Debugging and Troubleshooting

Deploying LangServe applications is generally straightforward, but issues can arise during development or in production. This chapter provides a detailed guide to identifying and resolving common errors, debugging LangChain workflows, and using best practices for efficient troubleshooting.

13.1 Common LangServe Errors and Their Fixes

Error 1: ModuleNotFoundError

- **Description**: This error occurs when a required Python module is not installed.

- **Cause**:

  - Missing or incorrectly installed dependencies.

- **Solution**:

  - Ensure all required dependencies are listed in requirements.txt and installed:

bash

```
pip install -r requirements.txt
```

  - Verify module installation:

bash

```
pip show langserve
```

Error 2: Invalid API Key

- **Description**: The API key for an external service, such as OpenAI, is missing or incorrect.

- **Cause**:

  - Incorrect API key in environment variables.

- **Solution**:

  - Verify the API key is set correctly in the .env file:

text
```
OPENAI_API_KEY=your_openai_api_key
```

  - Load environment variables in your application:

python
```
from dotenv import load_dotenv
load_dotenv()
```

Error 3: Address Already in Use

- **Description**: The specified port is being used by another process.

- **Cause**:

  - A previously running LangServe instance wasn't terminated properly.

- **Solution**:

  - Identify and terminate the process:

bash

```bash
lsof -i :8000
kill <process_id>
```

  o Use a different port:

bash

```bash
python app.py --port 8080
```

Error 4: Timeout Errors

- **Description**: API requests take too long to complete and exceed the timeout limit.

- **Cause**:

    o Complex LangChain workflows or insufficient resources.

- **Solution**:

    o Optimize the workflow logic (see Section 13.2).

    o Increase timeout settings:

bash

```bash
python app.py --timeout 60
```

Error 5: Schema Validation Failed

- **Description**: Input data does not match the expected schema.

- **Cause**:

- o Missing or incorrectly formatted input fields.

- **Solution**:

  - o Check the input schema using the /metadata endpoint:

bash

```
curl http://localhost:8000/metadata
```

  - o Adjust the input data to match the schema.

13.2 Debugging LangChain Workflows During Deployment

LangChain workflows form the core of LangServe applications. Debugging these workflows ensures they execute correctly during deployment.

Step 1: Test Locally Before Deployment

- Use Python scripts to test LangChain workflows in isolation:

python

```
from langchain import PromptTemplate, LLMChain


# Define a workflow

prompt =
PromptTemplate(input_variables=["query"],
template="Answer: {query}")
```

```
chain = LLMChain(prompt_template=prompt,
llm="openai-gpt3")


# Test the workflow

result = chain.run({"query": "What is
LangServe?"})

print(result)
```

Step 2: Enable Debug Logging

- Enable debug logs to get detailed insights into the workflow execution:

bash

```
python app.py --log-level debug
```

Example Debug Log:

css

```
2024-11-23 14:25:12 DEBUG: Received input:
{"query": "What is LangServe?"}

2024-11-23 14:25:12 DEBUG: Processed response:
"LangServe is a deployment tool for LangChain
workflows."
```

Step 3: Use LangSmith for Tracing

- Integrate LangSmith for visualizing workflow execution:

python

```
from langsmith.tracing import import enable_tracing

enable_tracing()
```

Step 4: Validate Workflow Inputs and Outputs

- Check if the workflow produces the expected results with test cases:

python

```
test_inputs = [{"query": "Define LangChain."},
{"query": "What is LangServe?"}]

for test_input in test_inputs:

    print(chain.run(test_input))
```

13.3 Tips for Quick Error Identification and Resolution

Efficient troubleshooting saves time and ensures smooth deployments. Below are tips for identifying and resolving issues quickly.

1. Monitor Logs

- **What to Look For**:

  o Error messages.

  o Unexpected behavior (e.g., slow execution, incorrect responses).

- **Tools**:

  o Terminal logs.

    o   LangSmith for visual debugging.

2. Use the /metadata Endpoint

- The /metadata endpoint provides details about the expected input and output schema:

bash

```
curl http://localhost:8000/metadata
```

Example Output:

json

```json
{
    "input_schema": {
        "query": "string"
    },
    "output_schema": {
        "response": "string"
    }
}
```

3. Isolate the Problem

- Test components (e.g., prompt templates, tools, memory) individually to narrow down the issue.

- Example:

python

```python
from langchain.prompts import PromptTemplate

prompt = PromptTemplate(template="What is
{subject}?", input_variables=["subject"])

print(prompt.format(subject="LangChain"))
```

4. Simplify the Workflow

- Remove unnecessary components to reduce complexity:

python

```python
# Start with a simple prompt

chain = LLMChain(prompt_template=prompt,
llm="openai-gpt3")
```

5. Handle Exceptions Gracefully

- Add error handling to catch and debug issues:

python

```python
try:
    result = chain.run({"query": "What is
LangServe?"})

except Exception as e:
    print(f"Error: {e}")
```

6. Document Common Errors

- Maintain a log of recurring issues and solutions for future reference.

7. Use Test Cases

- Write test scripts to validate workflow behavior:

python

```
def test_workflow():

    assert chain.run({"query": "What is
LangChain?"}) == "LangChain is a framework."
```

8. Regularly Update Dependencies

- Outdated libraries can cause compatibility issues:

bash

```
pip install --upgrade langserve langchain
```

9. Engage the Community

- Use forums, GitHub issues, and Slack channels to seek help for complex problems.

10. Monitor Resource Usage

- Ensure the server has adequate CPU and memory resources:

bash

```
top
```

This chapter has provided a comprehensive guide to debugging and troubleshooting LangServe applications. By understanding common errors, effectively debugging LangChain workflows, and following best practices for error resolution, you can minimize downtime and ensure robust deployments. With these skills, you are well-equipped to handle the challenges of deploying AI applications at scale.

Chapter 14: Performance Optimization

Performance optimization ensures that your LangServe APIs operate efficiently, with minimal latency and resource consumption, even under high loads. This chapter explores techniques to reduce API latency, optimize LangChain workflows, manage server resources, and fine-tune a high-performance API through a practical example.

14.1 Reducing API Latency

Latency is the time taken for an API request to be processed and the response returned. High latency can degrade user experience, especially for real-time applications like chatbots or streaming APIs.

Causes of High Latency

1. **Complex Workflows**:

   o Lengthy LangChain workflows with multiple components increase processing time.

2. **Large Inputs/Outputs**:

   o Handling large payloads consumes additional processing resources.

3. **Inefficient Resource Allocation**:

   o Insufficient server resources or suboptimal worker configuration can slow down requests.

Strategies to Reduce Latency

1. **Simplify Workflow Logic**

   o Minimize unnecessary steps in the workflow.

   o Example: Replace redundant prompts or unused components.

python

```python
from langchain import PromptTemplate, LLMChain

# Optimized prompt

prompt =
PromptTemplate(input_variables=["query"],
template="Answer: {query}")

chain = LLMChain(prompt_template=prompt,
llm="openai-gpt3")
```

2. **Enable Streaming Outputs**

   o Send partial responses incrementally for faster feedback.

python

```python
serve(chain, streaming=True)
```

3. **Use Caching**

   o Cache frequent queries to avoid redundant processing.

python

```python
from langchain.cache import InMemoryCache


# Enable caching
chain = LLMChain(prompt_template=prompt,
llm="openai-gpt3", cache=InMemoryCache())
```

4. **Optimize Input Data**

   o Preprocess or compress large inputs before sending
   them to the API.

5. **Increase Workers**

   o Allocate more workers to handle concurrent
   requests:

bash

```bash
python app.py --workers 4
```

6. **Use Faster Models**

   o Opt for smaller or domain-specific models with faster
   response times.

14.2 Optimizing LangChain Workflows for Better Performance

1. Reduce Workflow Complexity

- Combine multiple steps into a single operation where
  possible.

- Example: Simplify a multi-step question-answering process.

python

```
# Single-step prompt
prompt = PromptTemplate(
    input_variables=["question"],
    template="Provide a detailed answer to:
{question}"
)
```

2. Use Efficient Embeddings

- Select embeddings optimized for speed, such as lightweight models.

- Example:

python

```
from langchain.embeddings import
HuggingFaceEmbeddings


embeddings =
HuggingFaceEmbeddings(model_name="sentence-
transformers/all-MiniLM-L6-v2")
```

3. Limit Retrieval Scope

- Narrow the document search scope for vector-based retrieval.

- Example:

python

```
retriever =
vectorstore.as_retriever(search_kwargs={"k": 3})
# Return top 3 results
```

4. Parallelize Operations

- Process independent tasks in parallel to save time.

- Example:

python

```
import asyncio

async def process_queries(queries, chain):
    tasks = [chain.arun(query) for query in
queries]

    return await asyncio.gather(*tasks)


# Run tasks concurrently
asyncio.run(process_queries(["What is
LangChain?", "Define LangServe"], chain))
```

14.3 Managing Server Resources Efficiently

Efficient resource management is critical to sustaining high-performance APIs, especially under heavy traffic.

1. Optimize Worker Configuration

- Use multiple workers to handle concurrent requests efficiently:

bash

```
python app.py --workers 4
```

2. Monitor Resource Usage

- Use tools like htop or top to monitor CPU and memory usage.

3. Load Balancing

- Distribute traffic across multiple servers or instances using tools like NGINX:

nginx

```
http {
    upstream langserve_backend {
        server localhost:8000;
        server localhost:8001;
    }

    server {
        listen 80;
        location / {
            proxy_pass http://langserve_backend;
        }
    }
}
```

4. Autoscaling

- Enable autoscaling on cloud platforms to handle spikes in traffic automatically (e.g., AWS ECS, GCP).

5. Optimize Infrastructure

- Deploy on hardware with sufficient CPU and memory for your workload.

- Use GPU-based instances for compute-heavy tasks.

14.4 Example: Fine-Tuning a High-Performance API

This example demonstrates optimizing a chatbot API for high performance.

Objective

Optimize a customer support chatbot to handle 10,000 requests per minute with low latency.

Step 1: Define the Chatbot Workflow

Create a streamlined workflow:

python

```python
from langchain import PromptTemplate, LLMChain
from langserve import serve

# Define a simple and efficient prompt
prompt = PromptTemplate(
    input_variables=["query"],
```

```python
    template="Respond concisely to: {query}"
)


# Create the chatbot workflow
chain = LLMChain(prompt_template=prompt,
llm="openai-gpt3")


# Serve the workflow
if __name__ == "__main__":
    serve(chain)
```

Step 2: Enable Caching

Add caching to reduce redundant processing:

python

```python
from langchain.cache import InMemoryCache


chain = LLMChain(prompt_template=prompt,
llm="openai-gpt3", cache=InMemoryCache())
```

Step 3: Configure the Server

Optimize server configuration for high traffic:

bash

```bash
python chatbot.py --workers 8 --port 8080 --
timeout 30
```

Step 4: Deploy Load Balancing

Configure NGINX for load balancing:

nginx

```
http {
    upstream chatbot_backend {
        server localhost:8080;
        server localhost:8081;
    }

    server {
        listen 80;
        location / {
            proxy_pass http://chatbot_backend;
        }
    }
}
```

Step 5: Test Performance

Use Apache Benchmark to simulate traffic:

bash

```
ab -n 10000 -c 100 http://localhost/
```

Step 6: Monitor and Adjust

- Monitor resource usage with tools like htop.

- Scale up resources or optimize further based on results.

Performance optimization is crucial for ensuring responsive, scalable LangServe APIs. By reducing latency, optimizing LangChain workflows, and managing server resources efficiently, you can build APIs that perform well under heavy loads. The fine-tuning example illustrates how to apply these strategies in a real-world context, making your APIs robust and production-ready.

Chapter 15: Cost Optimization

Efficient cost management is crucial for deploying LangServe applications, particularly in cloud-based environments where expenses can scale quickly. This chapter covers strategies for managing costs, balancing performance with affordability, cost-saving tips for developers, and a practical example of deploying on a budget with minimal overhead.

15.1 Managing Costs in Cloud-Based Deployments

Cloud-based deployments offer flexibility and scalability but can also lead to high expenses if not managed carefully. Understanding cost structures and implementing best practices can significantly reduce spending.

Common Cloud Cost Components

Cost Component	Description	Examples
Compute Resources	Charges for virtual machines, containers, or serverless instances	AWS EC2, GCP Compute Engine, Azure VM
Storage	Costs for storing data, logs, and backups	AWS S3, GCP Storage, Azure Blob
Networking	Costs for data transfer between regions or external networks	Bandwidth and API calls
AI Model Usage	Costs for calling LLM APIs or training models	OpenAI, Hugging Face, Anthropic

Strategies to Manage Cloud Costs

1. **Select the Right Compute Resources**

   o Use smaller instance types for low-traffic applications.

   o Example: AWS T3 instances for development environments.

2. **Leverage Serverless Computing**

   o Use serverless platforms like AWS Lambda or GCP Cloud Functions for on-demand execution.

   o Benefits:

   ▪ No cost for idle instances.

   ▪ Scales automatically with demand.

3. **Use Spot Instances**

   o Spot instances provide significant cost savings but may be interrupted.

   o Example: Use AWS Spot Instances for non-critical workloads.

4. **Monitor Resource Usage**

   o Set up alerts to track CPU, memory, and storage usage to prevent over-provisioning.

   o Tools:

- AWS CloudWatch

- GCP Monitoring

- Azure Monitor

5. **Use Multi-Region Deployment Strategically**

    o Host your API in regions with lower costs if latency is acceptable.

15.2 Balancing Performance with Affordability

Balancing performance and affordability requires optimizing resource allocation without compromising user experience.

Optimization Techniques

1. **Right-Sizing Resources**

    o Provision instances based on actual traffic patterns.

    o Scale up for peak hours and scale down during off-hours.

2. **Load Balancing and Autoscaling**

    o Use load balancers to distribute traffic efficiently across instances.

    o Enable autoscaling to add or remove instances dynamically.

    o Example: AWS Application Load Balancer with Auto Scaling Group.

3. **Optimize LangChain Workflows**

- o Simplify workflows to reduce compute-intensive tasks.

- o Use lighter LLMs for cost-sensitive deployments.

4. **Caching**

- o Reduce redundant processing by caching frequent responses.

- o Example:

python

```
from langchain.cache import InMemoryCache


chain = LLMChain(prompt_template=prompt,
llm="openai-gpt3", cache=InMemoryCache())
```

5. **Prioritize Traffic**

- o Differentiate between high-priority and low-priority requests.

- o Example: Real-time queries processed immediately; batch jobs delayed to off-peak hours.

15.3 Cost-Saving Tips for Developers

1. Use Free or Low-Cost Tiers

- Leverage free usage tiers provided by cloud providers:

- AWS Free Tier: 750 hours of EC2 per month for the first 12 months.

- Google Cloud Free Tier: $300 in credits for new accounts.

2. Reserve Instances

- Reserve instances for predictable workloads to reduce long-term costs.

  - Example: AWS Reserved Instances offer savings of up to 75%.

3. Optimize Data Transfer

- Minimize cross-region and external data transfer to reduce networking costs.

- Example: Store data and host APIs in the same region.

4. Use Managed Services

- Use managed services like AWS Fargate or Azure Kubernetes Service (AKS) to offload maintenance and save operational costs.

5. Monitor and Analyze Costs

- Use cost analysis tools to track spending:

  - AWS Cost Explorer

  - GCP Billing Dashboard

  - Azure Cost Management

6. Leverage Open-Source Models

- Replace proprietary models with open-source alternatives to avoid API usage fees.

    - Example: Use Hugging Face models instead of paid LLMs when feasible.

7. Automate Scaling Policies

- Automate instance scaling to match workload demands.

bash

```
aws autoscaling set-desired-capacity --auto-
scaling-group-name myGroup --desired-capacity 2
```

8. Use Savings Plans

- Purchase cloud provider savings plans based on anticipated usage.

15.4 Example: Deploying on a Budget with Minimal Overhead

Objective

Deploy a LangServe-based chatbot API with a budget of $50 per month.

Step 1: Choose Cost-Effective Cloud Resources

- Select an AWS T3a.medium instance for hosting the API ($0.0416/hour).

Step 2: Enable Caching

Reduce processing costs by caching frequently asked queries:

python

```python
from langchain.cache import InMemoryCache


# Define workflow with caching

chain = LLMChain(prompt_template=prompt,
llm="openai-gpt3", cache=InMemoryCache())

serve(chain)
```

Step 3: Use Autoscaling

Configure autoscaling to maintain two instances during peak hours and one instance during off-hours:

1. **Setup Autoscaling Group**:

bash

```bash
aws autoscaling create-auto-scaling-group \
    --auto-scaling-group-name my-chatbot-group \
    --min-size 1 --max-size 3 --desired-capacity 2
```

2. **Define Scaling Policies**:

bash

```bash
aws autoscaling put-scaling-policy \
    --auto-scaling-group-name my-chatbot-group \
```

```
--policy-name ScaleOut \

--scaling-adjustment 1 \

--adjustment-type ChangeInCapacity
```

Step 4: Monitor and Optimize

1. Use AWS CloudWatch to monitor instance usage and performance.

2. Analyze cost trends in AWS Cost Explorer.

Step 5: Deploy and Test

Deploy the chatbot:

bash

```
python chatbot.py

Send requests to test the API:
```

bash

```
curl -X POST http://localhost:8000/invoke \

    -H "Content-Type: application/json" \

    -d '{"query": "What is the return policy?"}'
```

Budget Breakdown

Component	Monthly Cost

Component	Monthly Cost
AWS T3a.medium	$30 (2 instances, 300 hours)
Storage (AWS S3)	$5
Networking	$10
Total	$45

This chapter has explored cost optimization strategies for LangServe applications, including managing cloud-based deployment costs, balancing performance with affordability, and practical cost-saving tips for developers. The example deployment demonstrates how to deliver high-performance APIs within a constrained budget, ensuring efficient and sustainable operations.

Chapter 16: Deployment Readiness Checklist

Deploying a LangServe application requires thorough preparation to ensure functionality, scalability, and security in production environments. This chapter presents a detailed deployment readiness checklist, covering pre-deployment testing, scalability and security measures, API configuration finalization, and a practical checklist example for deploying a chatbot application.

16.1 Pre-Deployment Testing: What to Check

Thorough testing ensures the application behaves as expected under different scenarios. Below is a comprehensive list of tests to perform before deployment.

1. Functional Testing

- Verify that all workflows produce the correct outputs for various inputs.

- Example:

python

```python
from langchain import PromptTemplate, LLMChain

# Test the workflow

prompt =
PromptTemplate(input_variables=["query"],
template="Answer: {query}")

chain = LLMChain(prompt_template=prompt,
llm="openai-gpt3")
```

```
assert chain.run({"query": "What is LangServe?"})
== "LangServe is a deployment tool for LangChain
workflows."
```

2. Load Testing

- Simulate traffic to evaluate system performance under different loads.

- Tools: Apache Benchmark (AB), Locust, or JMeter.

- Example with Apache Benchmark:

bash

```
ab -n 1000 -c 100 http://localhost:8000/invoke
```

3. Integration Testing

- Test API integration with external systems (e.g., databases, authentication services).

- Example:

    o Verify database connections for a knowledge retrieval system.

4. Edge Case Testing

- Test how the application handles:

    o Large inputs.

    o Missing or invalid input data.

- Example:

bash

```
curl -X POST http://localhost:8000/invoke \
      -H "Content-Type: application/json" \
      -d '{}'
```

5. Error Handling

- Ensure graceful error messages for common issues.

- Example: Return a 400 Bad Request error for invalid input:

json

```
{
    "error": "Invalid input format. Please
provide a 'query' field."
}
```

6. End-to-End Testing

- Simulate real-world usage scenarios to validate the entire application flow.

16.2 Ensuring Scalability and Security Readiness

Scalability Checklist

Task	Action
Enable autoscaling	Configure autoscaling groups for dynamic traffic.

Task	Action
Load balancer setup	Use tools like NGINX or AWS Application Load Balancer to distribute traffic.
Optimize resource usage	Use efficient instance types and caching to minimize compute costs.
Database scaling	Ensure the database can handle concurrent read/write operations.

Security Checklist

Task	Action
Enable HTTPS	Use TLS certificates to encrypt API communication.
Implement API authentication	Require API keys or OAuth tokens for all requests.
Validate inputs	Sanitize and validate input data to prevent injection attacks.
Apply rate limiting	Use tools like slowapi to prevent abuse.
Monitor access logs	Track and analyze logs for suspicious activity.

Example: API Key Authentication

python

```python
from fastapi import Request, HTTPException

API_KEY = "your_api_key"

async def validate_api_key(request: Request):

    key = request.headers.get("x-api-key")

    if key != API_KEY:

        raise HTTPException(status_code=401,
detail="Unauthorized")
```

16.3 Finalizing API Configurations

Before deployment, ensure all configurations are optimized for production use.

1. Configure Environment Variables

- Store sensitive information (e.g., API keys, database credentials) securely in environment variables.

- Example .env file:

text

API_KEY=your_api_key

DATABASE_URL=your_database_url

2. Optimize Logging Levels

- Use info or warning levels in production to minimize verbose logging.

- Example:

bash

```bash
python app.py --log-level info
```

3. Set Timeouts

- Define appropriate timeouts for long-running requests:

bash

```bash
python app.py --timeout 30
```

4. Enable Monitoring Tools

- Integrate monitoring services like LangSmith, AWS CloudWatch, or Datadog to track application performance and errors.

5. Test Metadata Endpoint

- Verify that the /metadata endpoint correctly describes the input/output schema:

bash

```bash
curl http://localhost:8000/metadata
```

6. Validate Streaming Configuration

- Ensure streaming endpoints (/stream) are enabled for applications requiring real-time data:

python

```python
serve(chain, streaming=True)
```

16.4 Example: A Deployment Checklist for a Chatbot Application

Below is a practical deployment checklist tailored for a chatbot API.

Scenario

Deploying a customer support chatbot that handles up to 10,000 requests per day.

Checklist

1. **Pre-Deployment Testing**

   o Functional testing:

      - ☐ Input: "What is the return policy?"

      - ☐ Output: "Items can be returned within 30 days."

   o Load testing:

bash

```
ab -n 1000 -c 100 http://localhost:8000/invoke
```

   o Integration testing:

      - Verify database queries for product information.

   o Edge case testing:

      - ☐ Empty input.

- ▪ ☐ Large input (e.g., 1,000 characters).

2. **Scalability Readiness**

   o Autoscaling:

      ▪ Configured to handle 2 instances during peak hours.

   o Load balancing:

      ▪ NGINX configured with round-robin distribution.

3. **Security Readiness**

   o API key authentication:

bash

```
curl -X POST http://localhost:8000/invoke \
    -H "x-api-key: your_api_key" \
    -d '{"query": "What is the return policy?"}'
```

   o Rate limiting:

      ▪ Set to 10 requests per second per client.

4. **API Configuration**

   o Environment variables:

      ▪ ☐ API keys stored in .env file.

   o Logging level:

bash

```bash
python chatbot.py --log-level info
```

- o Timeout:

bash

```bash
python chatbot.py --timeout 30
```

5. **Monitoring and Metrics**

- o LangSmith tracing enabled for workflow analysis:

python

```python
from langsmith.tracing import enable_tracing
enable_tracing()
```

6. **Deployment Validation**

- o Test API endpoints:

  - /invoke: Returns valid responses.

  - /metadata: Shows accurate input/output schema.

  - /stream: Streams responses correctly.

A thorough deployment readiness checklist ensures that your LangServe application is functional, secure, and scalable. By testing workflows, configuring APIs, and validating security and performance, you can confidently deploy robust applications in production environments. The example deployment checklist for a chatbot illustrates how to apply these best practices in real-world scenarios.

Chapter 17: Integrating LangServe with Other Tools

LangServe is a powerful backend solution for deploying AI workflows, but its true potential is realized when integrated with other tools, such as front-end frameworks and external databases. This chapter explores connecting LangServe to modern front-end frameworks, linking it with external databases, and building a complete full-stack AI application.

17.1 Using LangServe with Popular Front-End Frameworks

Overview

Modern web applications often involve a front-end framework interacting with a backend API. LangServe APIs can seamlessly integrate with frameworks like React, Angular, and Vue.js to build interactive AI-powered user interfaces.

1. React

React is a JavaScript library for building user interfaces.

Example: Connecting LangServe to a React Application

Step 1: Set Up the React App

1. Create a new React app:

bash

```
npx create-react-app ai-chatbot
cd ai-chatbot
```

2. Install Axios for API calls:

bash

```bash
npm install axios
```

Step 2: Create a Chatbot Component

1. Add a Chatbot.js file:

javascript

```javascript
import React, { useState } from 'react';
import axios from 'axios';


const Chatbot = () => {
    const [query, setQuery] = useState('');
    const [response, setResponse] = useState('');


    const handleSubmit = async (e) => {
        e.preventDefault();
        try {
            const res = await
axios.post('http://localhost:8000/invoke', {
query });
            setResponse(res.data.response);
        } catch (error) {
            console.error('Error fetching
response:', error);
        }
```

```
    };


    return (
        <div>
            <h1>AI Chatbot</h1>
            <form onSubmit={handleSubmit}>
                <input
                    type="text"
                    value={query}
                    onChange={(e) =>
setQuery(e.target.value)}
                    placeholder="Ask
something..."
                />
                <button
type="submit">Send</button>
            </form>
            <p>Response: {response}</p>
        </div>
    );
};


export default Chatbot;
```

Step 3: Integrate the Component

1. Add the component to App.js:

javascript

```javascript
import React from 'react';
import Chatbot from './Chatbot';

function App() {
    return (
        <div className="App">
            <Chatbot />
        </div>
    );
}

export default App;
```

Step 4: Start the React App

bash

```bash
npm start
```

---

2. Angular

Angular is a TypeScript-based framework for building dynamic web applications.

Example: Connecting LangServe to an Angular Application

1. Set up an Angular project:

bash

```
ng new ai-chatbot
cd ai-chatbot
npm install axios
```

2. Create a chatbot service to interact with LangServe:

typescript

```typescript
import { Injectable } from '@angular/core';
import axios from 'axios';


@Injectable({
    providedIn: 'root'
})
export class ChatbotService {
    async getResponse(query: string):
Promise<string> {
        const response = await
axios.post('http://localhost:8000/invoke', {
query });

        return response.data.response;

    }

}
```

3. Create a chatbot component:

typescript

```typescript
import { Component } from '@angular/core';

import { ChatbotService } from
'./chatbot.service';


@Component({

    selector: 'app-chatbot',

    template: `

        <div>

            <h1>AI Chatbot</h1>

            <input [(ngModel)]="query"
placeholder="Ask something...">

            <button
(click)="sendQuery()">Send</button>

            <p>Response: {{response}}</p>

        </div>


})
export class ChatbotComponent {

    query: string = '';

    response: string = '';


    constructor(private chatbotService:
ChatbotService) {}
```

```
    async sendQuery() {
        this.response = await
this.chatbotService.getResponse(this.query);
    }
}
```

---

3. Vue.js

Vue.js is a progressive JavaScript framework for building UI applications.

Example: Connecting LangServe to a Vue.js Application

1. Set up a Vue.js app:

bash

```
vue create ai-chatbot
cd ai-chatbot
npm install axios
```

2. Create a chatbot component:

vue

```
<template>
    <div>
        <h1>AI Chatbot</h1>
        <input v-model="query" placeholder="Ask
something..." />
```

```
    <button @click="sendQuery">Send</button>
    <p>Response: {{ response }}</p>
  </div>
</template>

<script>
import axios from 'axios';

export default {
    data() {
        return {
            query: '',
            response: ''
        };
    },
    methods: {
        async sendQuery() {
            const res = await
axios.post('http://localhost:8000/invoke', {
query: this.query });
            this.response = res.data.response;
        }
    }
};
```

```
</script>
```

17.2 Connecting LangServe APIs with External Databases

LangServe can enhance its capabilities by integrating with external databases to store and retrieve data dynamically.

Database Options

Database	Use Case	Example
PostgreSQL	Structured data storage	User profiles, product catalogs
MongoDB	NoSQL for flexible schemas	Chat history, metadata
SQLite	Lightweight local storage	Prototyping, small-scale apps

Example: Integrating LangServe with PostgreSQL

Step 1: Install Dependencies

bash

```bash
pip install psycopg2
```

Step 2: Connect LangServe to the Database

python

```python
import psycopg2

from langchain.chains import LLMChain

from langserve import serve
```

```python
# Connect to PostgreSQL
conn = psycopg2.connect(
    dbname="your_db",
    user="your_user",
    password="your_password",
    host="localhost",
    port="5432"
)
```

```python
# Fetch data from the database
def fetch_data(query):
    with conn.cursor() as cursor:
        cursor.execute("SELECT response FROM knowledge_base WHERE query = %s", (query,))
        result = cursor.fetchone()
        return result[0] if result else "No data found."
```

```python
# Define LangChain workflow
llm_chain = LLMChain(prompt_template=None, llm="openai-gpt3", tools=[fetch_data])
```

```python
# Serve the application

if __name__ == "__main__":

    serve(llm_chain)
```

17.3 Example: Building a Full-Stack AI Application

Objective: Create a full-stack AI-powered Q&A system that integrates LangServe, PostgreSQL, and React.

1. Backend: LangServe with PostgreSQL

1. Set up the database with sample data:

sql

```sql
CREATE TABLE knowledge_base (

    id SERIAL PRIMARY KEY,

    query TEXT NOT NULL,

    response TEXT NOT NULL

);


INSERT INTO knowledge_base (query, response)

VALUES ('What is LangServe?', 'LangServe is a deployment tool for LangChain workflows.');
```

2. Connect LangServe to PostgreSQL as shown in Section 17.2.

2. Frontend: React

Use the React component described in Section 17.1 to interact with the LangServe API.

3. Deployment

1. **Backend Deployment**:

   o Deploy LangServe using AWS ECS or Azure App Service.

2. **Frontend Deployment**:

   o Deploy the React app using Netlify or Vercel.

This chapter demonstrates how LangServe can be integrated with front-end frameworks like React, Angular, and Vue.js, and external databases like PostgreSQL, MongoDB, and SQLite. The example of building a full-stack AI application illustrates how these integrations work together to create robust, scalable, and interactive AI-powered solutions.

Chapter 18: Automating LangServe Deployments

Automation is essential for efficient deployment and management of LangServe applications. This chapter explores creating CI/CD pipelines, using Docker and Kubernetes for automation, and provides a detailed example of setting up a CI/CD pipeline for LangServe.

18.1 CI/CD Pipelines for LangServe

Continuous Integration (CI) and Continuous Deployment (CD) pipelines streamline the process of building, testing, and deploying LangServe applications.

What Is CI/CD?

- **Continuous Integration (CI)**:

    o   Automatically builds and tests the application whenever code changes are pushed.

- **Continuous Deployment (CD)**:

    o   Automates the process of deploying changes to production.

Benefits for LangServe Applications

1. **Consistency**: Ensures all deployments follow the same process.

2. **Faster Delivery**: Automates repetitive tasks, reducing manual effort.

3. **Error Detection**: Quickly identifies and resolves issues with automated testing.

Example CI/CD Workflow

Step	Description
Code Commit	Developers push code to the version control system (e.g., GitHub).
Build	The pipeline builds the application, including dependencies.
Test	Automated tests validate functionality.
Deploy	The application is deployed to a staging or production environment.

Tools for CI/CD

Tool	Purpose	Example Use
GitHub Actions	CI/CD pipeline automation	Build, test, and deploy LangServe apps
Jenkins	Open-source automation server	Advanced CI/CD workflows
CircleCI	Cloud-based CI/CD	Automated deployment of containerized apps

18.2 Automating Deployment with Docker and Kubernetes

Docker and Kubernetes are widely used tools for containerization and orchestration, making LangServe applications portable and scalable.

Using Docker

Docker enables packaging LangServe applications with all dependencies into a container for consistent deployment.

Step 1: Create a Dockerfile

1. Add the following Dockerfile to your project:

dockerfile

```
# Use an official Python runtime as a parent image
FROM python:3.9-slim


# Set the working directory
WORKDIR /app


# Copy project files into the container
COPY . /app


# Install dependencies
RUN pip install --no-cache-dir -r requirements.txt
```

```
# Expose the port LangServe will run on
```

EXPOSE 8000

```
# Command to run the LangServe application
```

CMD ["python", "app.py"]

2. Build the Docker image:

bash

```
docker build -t langserve-app .
```

3. Run the Docker container:

bash

```
docker run -p 8000:8000 langserve-app
```

Using Kubernetes

Kubernetes orchestrates containerized applications, enabling scaling, load balancing, and high availability.

Step 1: Create Kubernetes Deployment

1. Define a deployment YAML file (deployment.yaml):

yaml

```yaml
apiVersion: apps/v1

kind: Deployment

metadata:

  name: langserve-app

spec:

  replicas: 3

  selector:

    matchLabels:

      app: langserve-app

  template:

    metadata:

      labels:

        app: langserve-app

    spec:

      containers:

      - name: langserve-app

        image: langserve-app:latest

        ports:

        - containerPort: 8000
```

2. Define a service YAML file (service.yaml):

yaml

```
apiVersion: v1
kind: Service
metadata:
  name: langserve-service
spec:
  selector:
    app: langserve-app
  ports:
    - protocol: TCP
      port: 80
      targetPort: 8000
  type: LoadBalancer
```

3. Deploy to Kubernetes:

bash

```bash
kubectl apply -f deployment.yaml
kubectl apply -f service.yaml
```

4. Verify the deployment:

bash

```bash
kubectl get pods
kubectl get services
```

18.3 Example: Setting Up a CI/CD Pipeline for LangServe

Scenario

Automate the build, test, and deployment process for a LangServe chatbot API using GitHub Actions.

Step 1: Create the LangServe Application

Save the following app.py as the LangServe application:

python

```python
from langchain import PromptTemplate, LLMChain
from langserve import serve


# Define the chatbot prompt
prompt = PromptTemplate(
    input_variables=["query"],
    template="Answer: {query}"
)
```

```python
# Create the LangChain workflow
chain = LLMChain(prompt_template=prompt,
llm="openai-gpt3")


# Serve the application
if __name__ == "__main__":
    serve(chain)
```

Step 2: Write the GitHub Actions Workflow

1. Add a .github/workflows/ci-cd.yml file:

yaml

```yaml
name: CI/CD Pipeline


on:
  push:
    branches:
      - main


jobs:
  build-and-test:
    runs-on: ubuntu-latest
```

```yaml
steps:

- name: Checkout code

  uses: actions/checkout@v3


- name: Set up Python

  uses: actions/setup-python@v3

  with:

    python-version: "3.9"


- name: Install dependencies

  run: |

    python -m pip install --upgrade pip

    pip install -r requirements.txt


- name: Run tests

  run: pytest


deploy:
```

```
needs: build-and-test

runs-on: ubuntu-latest

if: github.ref == 'refs/heads/main'


steps:
- name: Checkout code

  uses: actions/checkout@v3


- name: Log in to DockerHub

  uses: docker/login-action@v2

  with:

    username: ${{ secrets.DOCKER_USERNAME }}

    password: ${{ secrets.DOCKER_PASSWORD }}


- name: Build and push Docker image

  run: |

    docker build -t your-dockerhub-username/langserve-app:latest .

    docker push your-dockerhub-username/langserve-app:latest
```

```
- name: Deploy to Kubernetes

  run: |

    kubectl apply -f deployment.yaml

    kubectl apply -f service.yaml
```

2. Add secrets in the GitHub repository settings:

    o   DOCKER_USERNAME: Your DockerHub username.

    o   DOCKER_PASSWORD: Your DockerHub password.

Step 3: Test the CI/CD Pipeline

1. Push changes to the main branch:

bash

```
git add .

git commit -m "Add CI/CD pipeline"

git push origin main
```

2. Monitor the workflow execution on GitHub under the **Actions** tab.

Step 4: Verify Deployment

Access the LangServe API via the load balancer URL provided by Kubernetes:

bash

```
curl http://<load-balancer-url>/invoke \
    -H "Content-Type: application/json" \
    -d '{"query": "What is LangServe?"}'
```

Response:

json

```
{
    "response": "Answer: LangServe is a
deployment tool for LangChain workflows."
}
```

This chapter demonstrated how to automate LangServe deployments using CI/CD pipelines, Docker, and Kubernetes. The example CI/CD pipeline showcased how to build, test, and deploy a LangServe application efficiently, ensuring robust and scalable deployment practices. By automating deployment processes, developers can focus on innovation rather than repetitive tasks.

Chapter 19: Comparing LangServe with Other Deployment Tools

The landscape of AI deployment tools has expanded rapidly, offering a range of options for deploying machine learning and AI applications. LangServe is tailored specifically for LangChain workflows, but how does it stack up against other deployment tools? This chapter provides an in-depth comparison of LangServe's key features, strengths, weaknesses, and suitability for different AI applications. A detailed comparison chart highlights its position among competitors.

19.1 Key Features of LangServe vs. Competitors

LangServe distinguishes itself by focusing on **LangChain-based workflows**, offering streamlined deployment for applications built with LangChain. However, other deployment tools provide broader or alternative capabilities.

LangServe Key Features

Feature	Description
LangChain Integration	Native support for LangChain workflows, simplifying deployment.
REST API Endpoints	Automatic creation of /invoke, /batch, and /stream endpoints for synchronous and streaming use cases.
Ease of Use	Minimal setup required, making it ideal for developers with limited deployment expertise.

Feature	Description
Extensibility	Support for integrating middleware, external tools, and custom workflows.
Environment Agnostic	Works on cloud platforms, on-premises, or locally with containerization options.
Tracing with LangSmith	In-built tracing and debugging capabilities through LangSmith for visualizing workflows.

Comparison with Competitors

Tool	Key Features	Target Audience	Best Use Case
LangServe	Simplified LangChain deployment, RESTful APIs, streaming, native LangSmith integration	AI developers using LangChain	Deploying LangChain-powered chatbots and APIs
FastAPI	High-performance, web-based API framework, customizable endpoints	General API developers	Deploying REST APIs for any type of application
TensorFlow Serve	Model-serving platform for	Data scientists,	Serving TensorFlow or

Tool	Key Features	Target Audience	Best Use Case
	TensorFlow and Keras models, optimized for large-scale production	ML engineers	Keras models for predictions
TorchServe	Model-serving platform for PyTorch, supports custom handlers for preprocessing	PyTorch developers	Deploying PyTorch models with advanced preprocessing
Flask	Lightweight web framework, customizable API creation	Web developers, data scientists	Rapid prototyping of APIs for small-scale use cases
Ray Serve	Scalable model-serving library, multi-model support, integration with Ray for distributed computing	Scalable AI developers	Serving multiple models with distributed workloads
AWS SageMaker	Fully managed service for training, deploying, and scaling machine learning models	Enterprises, cloud users	Deploying AI models with auto-scaling on AWS

19.2 Strengths and Weaknesses of LangServe

Strengths

1. **Ease of Use**:

   ○ Simple configuration and deployment with minimal boilerplate.

   ○ Suitable for developers without extensive DevOps knowledge.

2. **Seamless LangChain Integration**:

   ○ Purpose-built for deploying LangChain workflows without additional modifications.

3. **Streaming Support**:

   ○ Built-in /stream endpoint for real-time responses.

4. **Tracing and Monitoring**:

   ○ Native integration with LangSmith for workflow tracing and debugging.

5. **Extensibility**:

   ○ Middleware support for adding custom validation, authentication, or pre/post-processing logic.

Weaknesses

1. **Limited Generalization**:

   ○ Focused primarily on LangChain workflows; not ideal for general-purpose APIs or non-LangChain AI models.

2. **Scaling Complexity**:

- While scalable, advanced orchestration (e.g., distributed serving) requires external tools like Kubernetes.

3. **Less Comprehensive Model Support**:

   - Unlike TensorFlow Serve or TorchServe, it doesn't cater to specific deep learning frameworks.

19.3 When to Choose LangServe for Your AI Application

LangServe is ideal for specific scenarios where simplicity and LangChain compatibility are critical. Below are considerations for choosing LangServe:

When to Use LangServe

1. **LangChain-Centric Applications**:

   - If your application is built around LangChain workflows, LangServe offers the most streamlined deployment.

2. **Quick Prototyping**:

   - Ideal for quickly deploying proof-of-concept applications with minimal setup.

3. **Streaming Applications**:

   - Built-in streaming support makes it perfect for chatbots and real-time data processing.

4. **Integration with LangSmith**:

- o If workflow tracing and monitoring are essential, LangServe's native LangSmith support is a major advantage.

When to Consider Alternatives

1. **Multi-Model Serving**:

   - o For serving multiple models simultaneously, tools like Ray Serve or TensorFlow Serve are better suited.

2. **Non-LangChain Applications**:

   - o For general-purpose AI APIs, consider frameworks like FastAPI or Flask.

3. **Highly Scalable Workloads**:

   - o For large-scale distributed workloads, AWS SageMaker or Ray Serve might be more appropriate.

19.4 Example: A Comparison Chart for AI Deployment Tools

Feature	LangServe	FastAPI	TensorFlow Serve	Torch Serve	Ray Serve	AWS SageMaker
Primary Use Case	LangChain workflows	General REST APIs	TensorFlow/Keras models	PyTorch models	Distributed serving	Managed AI serving
Ease of Use	□□□□□	□□□□□	□□□	□□□	□□□□	□□□□
Strea	□	□	□	□	□	□

Feature	LangServe	FastAPI	TensorFlow Serve	Torch Serve	Ray Serve	AWS SageMaker
ming Support						
Multi-Model Support	☐	☐	☐	☐	☐	☐
Tracing and Monitoring	☐ (LangSmith)	☐	☐	☐	☐	☐
Integration with AI Tools	LangChain, LangSmith	Open-ended	TensorFlow/Keras	PyTorch	Open-ended	Open-ended
Scaling	Manual/External tools	Manual/External tools	Built-in	Built-in	Distributed	Auto-scaling
Best For	LangChain workflows	Small APIs	TensorFlow/Keras users	PyTorch users	Distributed apps	Cloud enterprises

LangServe excels in simplicity and LangChain-specific capabilities, making it an excellent choice for AI applications built on LangChain workflows. However, for general-purpose AI deployments, tools like FastAPI, TensorFlow Serve, or AWS SageMaker may be better suited. The comparison chart highlights LangServe's strengths and helps developers choose the right tool for their specific use case. By understanding these differences, you can make informed decisions to optimize your deployment strategy.

Chapter 20: The Future of AI Deployment

As artificial intelligence continues to reshape industries, the deployment of AI applications is evolving rapidly. This chapter explores emerging trends in AI deployment, the evolving role of LangServe and LangChain, strategies for preparing for future deployment technologies, and how developers can leverage LangServe to innovate and stay ahead of the curve.

20.1 Emerging Trends in AI Application Deployment

The landscape of AI application deployment is shifting with advancements in technology and changing user demands. Below are the key trends shaping the future of AI deployment.

1. Real-Time AI Applications

- **Trend**: Increased demand for real-time AI applications such as chatbots, live translations, and predictive analytics.

- **Implication**: Deployment tools must support low-latency, high-throughput streaming capabilities.

- **Example**:

    o LangServe's /stream endpoint facilitates real-time data processing.

2. Multi-Modal AI

- **Trend**: AI applications integrating text, images, audio, and video processing in a single workflow.

- **Implication**: Deployment platforms will need to support multi-modal models and workflows.

- **Example**:

    o Combining LangChain's text-based capabilities with computer vision APIs for enhanced applications.

3. Serverless and Edge Computing

- **Trend**: Shift toward serverless architectures and edge deployments to reduce latency and improve scalability.

- **Implication**: Tools like LangServe may evolve to offer edge deployment options.

- **Example**:

    o Deploying LangServe APIs on serverless platforms like AWS Lambda or edge platforms like Cloudflare Workers.

4. AutoML and Model Customization

- **Trend**: Simplified tools for training and customizing models with minimal expertise.

- **Implication**: Deployment platforms will integrate with AutoML tools to support end-to-end workflows.

- **Example**:

    o Integrating LangServe with platforms like Google AutoML for seamless model deployment.

5. Emphasis on Sustainability

- **Trend**: Reducing the environmental impact of AI deployments through efficient resource utilization.

- **Implication**: Deployment platforms must optimize resource usage and support green computing practices.

20.2 The Evolving Role of LangServe and LangChain

LangServe and LangChain are positioned to play a significant role in the future of AI deployment, particularly for applications requiring complex workflows and real-time processing.

LangServe's Contributions

1. **Streamlined Deployment**:

   o LangServe simplifies deploying LangChain workflows, making AI accessible to developers with minimal DevOps experience.

2. **Focus on Real-Time Capabilities**:

   o Built-in support for streaming endpoints positions LangServe as a go-to tool for real-time AI applications.

3. **Integration with Observability Tools**:

   o LangSmith integration offers unparalleled insights into workflow performance and debugging.

LangChain's Contributions

1. **Workflow Orchestration**:

- LangChain provides a modular approach to building complex AI applications by chaining together models, prompts, and tools.

2. **Versatility**:

    - Support for various use cases, from question-answering systems to document retrieval and beyond.

Future Directions

- **Advanced Features**:

    - Adding support for multi-modal workflows and enhanced security features.

- **Expanding Ecosystem**:

    - Collaboration with cloud providers, AutoML platforms, and edge computing services.

- **Open Source Innovations**:

    - Growing the community around LangChain and LangServe to foster innovation and address user needs.

20.3 Preparing for the Next Wave of Deployment Technologies

As deployment technologies evolve, developers and organizations must adapt to remain competitive. Below are strategies to prepare for the future.

1. Stay Updated with Emerging Technologies

- Follow industry trends and innovations in deployment platforms, containerization, and edge computing.

- Resources:

  - Blogs, webinars, and community forums for tools like LangChain, Kubernetes, and AWS.

2. Embrace Automation

- Automate deployment pipelines with CI/CD tools to streamline workflows and reduce errors.

- Example:

yaml

```yaml
name: LangServe CI/CD

on: push:
  branches: [main]

jobs:
  deploy:
    runs-on: ubuntu-latest
    steps:
```

```
- name: Checkout code

  uses: actions/checkout@v3

- name: Build and deploy

  run: |

    docker build -t langserve-app .

    docker push your-registry/langserve-app

    kubectl apply -f deployment.yaml
```

3. Adopt Scalable Architectures

- Implement scalable systems using container orchestration
  tools like Kubernetes or serverless platforms like AWS
  Lambda.

4. Optimize for Cost and Sustainability

- Use tools to monitor resource usage and reduce waste.

- Example:

  - Implementing auto-scaling policies in Kubernetes to
    dynamically adjust resource allocation.

5. Focus on Security

- Integrate authentication, encryption, and rate limiting into
  deployment workflows to ensure robust security.

20.4 Encouraging Readers to Innovate with LangServe

LangServe offers a flexible and powerful platform for deploying AI workflows. Below are ways developers can leverage LangServe for innovation:

1. Experiment with New Use Cases

- Combine LangChain workflows with external tools and APIs to explore novel applications.

- Example:

  - Integrating a LangServe chatbot API with IoT devices for voice-controlled automation.

2. Build Scalable, Real-Time Applications

- Use LangServe's streaming capabilities to create applications like:

  - Real-time sentiment analysis for social media.

  - Live customer support chatbots.

3. Contribute to the Ecosystem

- Extend LangServe with custom middleware or plugins.

- Participate in open-source projects to help shape the tool's future.

4. Collaborate Across Disciplines

- Use LangServe as a bridge between AI developers, DevOps teams, and end-users.

- Example:

  - Deploying an AI-powered decision-support system in collaboration with business analysts.

The future of AI deployment is exciting, with emerging trends like real-time applications, multi-modal AI, serverless computing, and sustainable practices shaping the industry. LangServe and LangChain are well-positioned to play pivotal roles in this transformation. By staying informed, embracing automation, and innovating with LangServe, developers can lead the next wave of AI deployment technologies, creating impactful and scalable solutions. This chapter concludes by encouraging readers to explore the full potential of LangServe and drive innovation in their AI projects.

Appendix A: LangServe API Reference

This appendix provides a comprehensive guide to the LangServe API, covering the details of its endpoints, input and output schema formats, and the supported LangChain workflows. This reference is intended to help developers utilize LangServe to its fullest potential.

A.1 Detailed Documentation of LangServe Endpoints

LangServe automatically creates RESTful endpoints to interact with your LangChain workflows. Below are the main endpoints and their functionalities.

1. /invoke Endpoint

- **Purpose**: Handles single synchronous requests and provides a complete response.

- **Method**: POST

- **URL**: /invoke

Request Format:

json

```
{
  "query": "What is LangServe?"
}
```

Response Format:

json

```
{

  "response": "LangServe is a deployment tool for
LangChain workflows."

}
```

Example Using curl:

bash

```
curl -X POST http://localhost:8000/invoke \

    -H "Content-Type: application/json" \

    -d '{"query": "What is LangServe?"}'
```

2. /batch Endpoint

- **Purpose**: Processes multiple inputs in a single request, returning a batch of results.

- **Method**: POST

- **URL**: /batch

Request Format:

json

```
{

  "queries": [

    "What is LangServe?",

    "Explain LangChain."
```

```
    ]

}
```

Response Format:

json

```
{

  "responses": [

    "LangServe is a deployment tool for LangChain
workflows.",

    "LangChain is a framework for building AI
workflows."

  ]

}
```

Example Using curl:

bash

```
curl -X POST http://localhost:8000/batch \

    -H "Content-Type: application/json" \

    -d '{"queries": ["What is LangServe?",
"Explain LangChain."]}'
```

3. /stream Endpoint

- **Purpose**: Streams responses incrementally, ideal for real-time applications.

- **Method**: POST

- **URL**: /stream

Request Format:

json

```
{
  "query": "What is LangServe?"
}
```

Response Format:

csharp

```
LangServe

is

a

deployment

tool

for

LangChain

workflows.
```

Example Using curl:

bash

```
curl -X POST http://localhost:8000/stream \
    -H "Content-Type: application/json" \
    -d '{"query": "What is LangServe?"}'
```

4. /metadata Endpoint

- **Purpose**: Provides details about the input and output schema for the deployed application.

- **Method**: GET

- **URL**: /metadata

Response Format:

json

```
{
  "input_schema": {
    "query": "string"
  },
  "output_schema": {
    "response": "string"
  }
}
```

Example Using curl:

bash

curl http://localhost:8000/metadata

A.2 Input and Output Schema Formats

LangServe requires a clear definition of input and output formats for your LangChain workflows. These schemas are automatically generated based on the workflow's structure.

Input Schema

Field	Type	Description
query	string	The input text or prompt provided to the API.
context	object	(Optional) Additional context for processing.

Example:

json

```
{

  "query": "What is LangChain?",

  "context": {

    "user_id": 1234,

    "session_id": "abc-xyz"

  }

}
```

Output Schema

Field	Type	Description
response	string	The generated output from the LangChain workflow.

Example:

json

```json
{

  "response": "LangChain is a framework for building AI workflows."

}
```

Batch Schema

Field	Type	Description
queries	array[string]	A list of inputs to be processed.
responses	array[string]	A list of corresponding outputs.

A.3 Supported LangChain Workflows

LangServe supports deploying various LangChain workflows, enabling versatile AI applications.

1. Question-Answering Workflow

- **Description**: Processes a question and retrieves an answer from a knowledge base.

- **Example**:

python

```python
from langchain import RetrievalQA, FAISS, OpenAIEmbeddings

from langserve import serve
```

```python
# Load the knowledge base
vectorstore = FAISS.load_local("./vectorstore")
retriever = vectorstore.as_retriever()

# Define the QA workflow
qa_chain = RetrievalQA(retriever=retriever)

# Serve the workflow
if __name__ == "__main__":
    serve(qa_chain)
```

2. Conversational Agent

- **Description**: Maintains a conversation with memory and context.

- **Example**:

python

```python
from langchain import ConversationChain, OpenAI, Memory
from langserve import serve

# Define memory
memory = Memory()
```

```python
# Create conversational workflow
chain = ConversationChain(llm=OpenAI("gpt-3"),
memory=memory)


# Serve the application
if __name__ == "__main__":
    serve(chain)
```

3. Summarization Workflow

- **Description**: Summarizes long text into concise outputs.

- **Example**:

python
```python
from langchain import SummarizationChain
from langserve import serve


# Create summarization workflow
chain = SummarizationChain(llm="openai-gpt3")


# Serve the workflow
if __name__ == "__main__":
    serve(chain)
```

4. Custom Workflows

- **Description**: LangServe supports custom workflows combining multiple tools and prompts.

- **Example**:

python

```python
from langchain import LLMChain, PromptTemplate
from langserve import serve


# Define a custom prompt
prompt =
PromptTemplate(input_variables=["query"],
template="Answer: {query}")


# Create a custom workflow
chain = LLMChain(prompt_template=prompt,
llm="openai-gpt3")


# Serve the application
if __name__ == "__main__":
    serve(chain)
```

This appendix provides a detailed overview of LangServe's endpoints, schema formats, and supported workflows, serving as a quick reference for developers deploying LangChain-based AI applications. By leveraging the power of LangServe's API and its seamless integration with LangChain, developers can deploy versatile and scalable AI solutions efficiently.

Appendix B: Tools and Libraries

This appendix provides an overview of the tools and libraries used throughout this book and additional resources to enhance your work with LangChain and LangServe. These tools cover essential functionalities, from workflow development to deployment and optimization.

B.1 Overview of Tools Used in the Book

Below is a detailed list of the tools introduced and utilized in this book, organized by their role in AI application development and deployment.

1. LangChain

- **Purpose**: Framework for building AI workflows by chaining together language models, prompts, tools, and memory.

- **Key Features**:

    o   Workflow orchestration.

    o   Integration with knowledge retrieval tools.

    o   Modular components for flexible designs.

- **Example Use**:

python

```
from langchain import PromptTemplate, LLMChain
```

```
prompt =
PromptTemplate(input_variables=["query"],
template="Answer: {query}")

chain = LLMChain(prompt_template=prompt,
llm="openai-gpt3")
```

2. LangServe

- **Purpose**: Deployment tool for LangChain workflows, offering RESTful API endpoints and real-time streaming support.

- **Key Features**:

    o Simplifies deployment with minimal configuration.

    o Supports streaming via /stream endpoint.

    o Native integration with LangSmith for monitoring.

- **Example Use**:

python

```
from langserve import serve

if __name__ == "__main__":

    serve(chain)
```

3. LangSmith

- **Purpose**: Tracing and debugging tool for LangChain workflows.

- **Key Features**:

    o Visualize execution flow.

      ○ Monitor latency and performance.

- **Example Use**:

python

```
from langsmith.tracing import enable_tracing

enable_tracing()
```

4. Docker

- **Purpose**: Containerization platform for packaging and deploying LangServe applications with all dependencies.

- **Key Features**:

      ○ Consistent runtime across environments.

      ○ Simplifies deployment in Kubernetes or cloud platforms.

- **Example Dockerfile**:

dockerfile

```
FROM python:3.9-slim

WORKDIR /app

COPY . /app

RUN pip install -r requirements.txt

CMD ["python", "app.py"]
```

5. Kubernetes

- **Purpose**: Orchestration platform for managing containerized LangServe applications.

- **Key Features**:

  - Autoscaling for handling variable loads.

  - Ensures high availability with replicas.

- **Example Deployment YAML**:

yaml

```
apiVersion: apps/v1
kind: Deployment
metadata:
  name: langserve-app
spec:
  replicas: 3
  selector:
    matchLabels:
      app: langserve-app
  template:
    metadata:
      labels:
        app: langserve-app
    spec:
      containers:
```

```
- name: langserve-app

  image: langserve-app:latest

  ports:

  - containerPort: 8000
```

6. GitHub Actions

- **Purpose**: Automates CI/CD pipelines for LangServe applications.

- **Key Features**:

  - Automates testing, building, and deploying.

  - Integrates seamlessly with Docker and Kubernetes.

- **Example Workflow**:

yaml

```
name: LangServe CI/CD


on: push:

  branches:

    - main
```

jobs:

  deploy:

   runs-on: ubuntu-latest

```
steps:

- name: Checkout code

  uses: actions/checkout@v3

- name: Build and deploy

  run: |

    docker build -t langserve-app .

    docker push your-repo/langserve-app

    kubectl apply -f deployment.yaml
```

B.2 Additional Libraries and Frameworks for LangChain and LangServe

While LangChain and LangServe are the primary tools for developing and deploying workflows, several libraries and frameworks can enhance their capabilities.

1. FastAPI

- **Purpose**: High-performance web framework for building APIs.

- **Use Case**: Extend LangServe APIs with custom routes or additional endpoints.

- **Example**:

python

```python
from fastapi import FastAPI

app = FastAPI()

@app.get("/")
def read_root():
    return {"message": "Welcome to LangServe"}
```

2. TensorFlow and PyTorch

- **Purpose**: Popular deep learning frameworks for building and training machine learning models.

- **Use Case**: Incorporate custom ML models into LangChain workflows.

- **Example with PyTorch**:

python

```python
import torch

model = torch.load("model.pth")
def predict(input_data):
    return model(input_data)
```

3. Hugging Face Transformers

- **Purpose**: Library for pre-trained transformer models, such as BERT, GPT, and T5.

- **Use Case**: Use Hugging Face models as part of LangChain workflows.

- **Example**:

python

```
from transformers import pipeline

summarizer = pipeline("summarization")

print(summarizer("LangServe simplifies deployment
of LangChain workflows."))
```

4. Psycopg2

- **Purpose**: PostgreSQL adapter for Python.

- **Use Case**: Connect LangServe applications to PostgreSQL databases for dynamic data retrieval.

- **Example**:

python

```
import psycopg2

conn = psycopg2.connect("dbname=test
user=postgres")

cur = conn.cursor()

cur.execute("SELECT * FROM my_table")

print(cur.fetchall())
```

5. Redis

- **Purpose**: In-memory data store for caching and message brokering.

- **Use Case**: Cache frequent queries in LangServe workflows for improved performance.

- **Example**:

python

```
import redis

r = redis.Redis(host='localhost', port=6379,
db=0)

r.set("key", "value")

print(r.get("key"))
```

6. Pandas

- **Purpose**: Data analysis and manipulation library.

- **Use Case**: Process structured data within LangChain workflows.

- **Example**:

python

```
import pandas as pd

df = pd.read_csv("data.csv")

print(df.head())
```

7. OpenAI API

- **Purpose**: Access OpenAI's GPT models for text generation.

- **Use Case**: Use GPT models as the LLM in LangChain workflows.

- **Example**:

python

```python
import openai

openai.api_key = "your-api-key"

response = openai.Completion.create(
    model="text-davinci-003",
    prompt="What is LangServe?",
    max_tokens=50
)

print(response.choices[0].text)
```

Summary Table of Tools

Tool/Library	Purpose	Integration
LangChain	Workflow orchestration	Core of all workflows
LangServe	Deployment of LangChain workflows	RESTful APIs and streaming
LangSmith	Debugging and tracing	Monitoring and performance
Docker	Containerization	Consistent deployments
Kubernetes	Orchestration	Scaling and availability

Tool/Library	Purpose	Integration
FastAPI	API development	Extend LangServe capabilities
Psycopg2	PostgreSQL integration	Dynamic database queries
Redis	Caching	Performance optimization
Hugging Face Transformers	Pre-trained models for NLP tasks	Enhanced AI workflows
OpenAI API	GPT models for text generation	Core language processing
TensorFlow and PyTorch	Custom deep learning models	Advanced AI workflows

This appendix provides a detailed overview of the tools and libraries that power LangChain and LangServe workflows, along with additional resources to enhance functionality. Whether you are building a chatbot, knowledge retrieval system, or a real-time streaming API, these tools will help you extend the capabilities of LangServe and deploy scalable, efficient AI applications.

Appendix C: Troubleshooting Checklist

This appendix serves as a quick reference for diagnosing and solving common issues encountered when using LangServe. Whether you're experiencing errors during setup, deployment, or runtime, this checklist provides step-by-step guidance to resolve the most frequent challenges.

C.1 Quick Reference for Solving Common LangServe Issues

The table below summarizes common LangServe issues, their causes, and step-by-step solutions.

Issue	Cause	Solution
ModuleNotFoundError	Required modules or dependencies are not installed.	1. Ensure all dependencies are listed in requirements.txt.
		2. Run: pip install -r requirements.txt.
		3. Verify installation with: pip show <module_name>.
Invalid API Key	Missing or incorrect API key for external services like	1. Check the .env file or environment variables for the correct API key.

Issue	Cause	Solution
	OpenAI.	
		2. Load environment variables using dotenv:
		``python
		from dotenv import load_dotenv
		load_dotenv()
		``
Address Already in Use	Port conflict because another process is using the specified port.	1. Find the conflicting process: lsof -i :8000.
		2. Terminate the process: kill <process_id>.
		3. Run LangServe on a different port: python app.py --port 8080.
Timeout Errors	Requests take too long to process due to complex	1. Optimize LangChain workflows to simplify processing.

Issue	Cause	Solution
	workflows or insufficient server resources.	
		2. Increase timeout settings: python app.py --timeout 60.
		3. Use more powerful server hardware or scale resources.
Input Schema Validation Failed	Input data does not match the expected schema.	1. Check the schema using the /metadata endpoint:
		``bash
		curl http://localhost:8000/metadata
		``
		2. Adjust input format to match the schema requirements.
		Example schema:
		``json

Issue	Cause	Solution
		{
		"input_schema": { "query": "string" }
		}
		``
LangServe Server Crashes	Uncaught exceptions in LangChain workflows.	1. Wrap LangChain workflows in try-except blocks:
		``python
		try:
		response = chain.run({"query": "What is LangServe?"})
		except Exception as e:
		print(f"Error: {e}")
		``
		2. Debug with detailed logs by setting log level to debug:

Issue	Cause	Solution
		``bash
		python app.py --log-level debug
		``
Batch Processing Issues	Errors occur when processing multiple inputs simultaneously.	1. Validate the batch input format:
		``json
		{ "queries": ["What is LangServe?", "Explain LangChain."] }
		``
		2. Test the batch endpoint manually using curl to identify issues.
		``bash
		curl -X POST http://localhost:8000/batch -H "Content-Type:

Issue	Cause	Solution
		application/json" -d '{"queries": ["Question1", "Question2"]}'
		``
Streaming Endpoint Errors	Responses are not streamed correctly or arrive incomplete.	1. Verify the streaming configuration in the LangServe deployment script:
		``python
		serve(chain, streaming=True)
		``
		2. Test the /stream endpoint manually using curl:
		``bash
		curl -X POST http://localhost:8000/stream -H "Content-Type: application/json" -d '{"query": "Test"}'
		``

Issue	Cause	Solution
Deployment Issues with Docker	LangServe fails to start or behaves unexpectedly in a Docker container.	1. Verify that the Docker container builds successfully:
		``bash
		docker build -t langserve-app .
		``
		2. Check container logs for errors:
		``bash
		docker logs <container_id>
		``
		3. Ensure the correct CMD is specified in the Dockerfile:
		``dockerfile
		CMD ["python", "app.py"]
		``

Issue	Cause	Solution
Resource Exhaustion During High Traffic	Insufficient CPU, memory, or workers to handle concurrent requests.	1. Increase the number of workers:
		``bash
		python app.py --workers 4
		``
		2. Monitor resource usage with tools like htop or Kubernetes dashboards.

This troubleshooting checklist serves as a quick reference for diagnosing and resolving common LangServe issues. By systematically identifying the cause and applying the suggested solutions, you can ensure smooth deployment and operation of your LangServe applications. Proper logging, schema validation, and resource management will further minimize disruptions and improve overall performance.

Appendix D: Deployment Readiness Checklist

Ensuring that your LangServe application is deployment-ready requires careful preparation. This appendix provides a comprehensive checklist to finalize your application before going live and strategies to ensure robustness in production environments. By following these steps, you can reduce downtime, enhance security, and deliver a seamless user experience.

D.1 Final Steps Before Going Live

1. Validate Application Functionality

- **Unit Tests**:

    o   Ensure each LangChain workflow behaves as expected under various inputs.

python

```python
from langchain import PromptTemplate, LLMChain

prompt =
PromptTemplate(input_variables=["query"],
template="Answer: {query}")

chain = LLMChain(prompt_template=prompt,
llm="openai-gpt3")


assert chain.run({"query": "What is LangServe?"})
== "LangServe is a deployment tool for LangChain
workflows."
```

- **Integration Tests**:

    - Test end-to-end workflows to ensure all components (e.g., databases, external APIs) work together seamlessly.

- **Functional Tests**:

    - Validate that API endpoints produce correct results for real-world use cases.

2. Perform Load Testing

- Use tools like Apache Benchmark (AB) or Locust to simulate high-traffic scenarios.

- Example with Apache Benchmark:

bash

```
ab -n 1000 -c 100 http://localhost:8000/invoke
```

- Analyze metrics like:

    - Response times.

    - Throughput (requests per second).

    - Failure rates.

3. Optimize API Performance

- **Caching**:

    - Implement caching for frequent queries to reduce processing time.

python

```
from langchain.cache import InMemoryCache
```

```
chain = LLMChain(prompt_template=prompt,
llm="openai-gpt3", cache=InMemoryCache())
```

- **Batching**:

    o   Use the /batch endpoint for processing multiple requests simultaneously to improve efficiency.

- **Streaming**:

    o   Enable the /stream endpoint for applications requiring real-time responses:

python

```
serve(chain, streaming=True)
```

4. Finalize Configuration

- **Environment Variables**:

    o   Store sensitive information such as API keys and database credentials securely in environment variables.

text

OPENAI_API_KEY=your_api_key

DATABASE_URL=your_database_url

- **Logging**:

  - Set appropriate log levels (info, warning) for production environments:

bash

```
python app.py --log-level info
```

- **Timeouts**:

  - Configure timeouts to prevent hanging requests:

bash

```
python app.py --timeout 30
```

5. Security Checks

- **Authentication**:

  - Require API keys or OAuth tokens for access.

python

```
from fastapi import Request, HTTPException
async def validate_api_key(request: Request):
    key = request.headers.get("x-api-key")
    if key != "your_api_key":
        raise HTTPException(status_code=401,
detail="Unauthorized")
```

- **Rate Limiting**:

  - Implement rate limiting to prevent abuse:

bash

```
pip install slowapi
```

- **Input Validation**:

  - Validate all incoming requests to avoid injection attacks.

- **HTTPS**:

  - Use HTTPS to encrypt communication between clients and servers.

D.2 Ensuring Robustness in Production Environments

1. Scalability

- **Autoscaling**:

  - Configure autoscaling to handle spikes in traffic:

bash

```
kubectl autoscale deployment langserve-app --cpu-
percent=80 --min=1 --max=10
```

- **Load Balancing**:

  - Use a load balancer to distribute traffic evenly across instances:

nginx

```
upstream langserve_backend {

    server localhost:8000;

    server localhost:8001;

}


server {

    listen 80;

    location / {

        proxy_pass http://langserve_backend;

    }

}
```

2. Monitoring and Observability

- **LangSmith Tracing**:

    o Enable LangSmith tracing to monitor workflow
       performance and latency:

python
```
from langsmith.tracing import enable_tracing

enable_tracing()
```

- **Logs and Metrics**:

    o Set up centralized logging using tools like ELK Stack
       (Elasticsearch, Logstash, Kibana) or AWS
       CloudWatch.

- **Health Checks**:

  o Implement health checks to ensure the API is running:

bash

```
curl http://localhost:8000/health
```

3. High Availability

- **Replicas**:

  o Deploy multiple replicas of your application to ensure availability.

  o Example Kubernetes configuration:

yaml

```
spec:
  replicas: 3
```

- **Disaster Recovery**:

  o Set up automatic backups for critical data and configurations.

4. Resource Optimization

- **Right-Sizing Instances**:

  o Choose instance types based on your workload.

- Example: Use t3.medium for low traffic and m5.large for higher traffic.

- **Database Optimization**:

  - Index frequently queried fields to improve database performance.

- **Efficient Memory Usage**:

  - Monitor memory usage and optimize workflows to reduce overhead.

5. Regular Updates

- **Dependencies**:

  - Keep LangChain, LangServe, and other dependencies up to date:

bash

```
pip install --upgrade langserve langchain
```

- **Application Code**:

  - Schedule regular reviews and updates to ensure compatibility with new frameworks or APIs.

Final Deployment Checklist

Task	Status	Notes
Functional Testing	☐	All workflows validated with expected inputs and outputs.

Task	Status	Notes
Load Testing	☐	Handled 1,000 requests per second with <5% failure rate.
Performance Optimization	☐	Implemented caching, batching, and streaming where applicable.
Configuration Finalization	☐	Environment variables, logging, and timeouts configured correctly.
Security Measures	☐	API keys, rate limiting, input validation, and HTTPS enabled.
Scalability Setup	☐	Autoscaling and load balancing configured for peak traffic.
Monitoring and Health Checks	☐	LangSmith tracing enabled; health checks deployed.
High Availability	☐	Application replicated across 3 instances.
Resource Optimization	☐	Efficient use of compute, database, and memory resources.
Regular Update Plan	☐	Scheduled monthly reviews for dependencies and application code.

This deployment readiness checklist ensures your LangServe application is robust, secure, and scalable before going live. By validating functionality, optimizing performance, and implementing best practices for security and monitoring, you can deliver reliable and efficient AI applications in production environments.

Appendix E: Resources for Further Learning

This appendix provides a curated list of resources to help you deepen your understanding of LangServe, LangChain, and the broader ecosystem of AI application development and deployment. These resources include official documentation, recommended books and courses, as well as community forums and repositories to stay connected with the AI community.

E.1 Official LangServe and LangChain Documentation

LangServe Documentation

- **URL**: LangServe Documentation

- **Overview**:

  o Comprehensive guide for deploying LangChain workflows with LangServe.

  o Topics include setup, API configuration, streaming, and troubleshooting.

- **Key Sections**:

  o Quick Start Guide: Rapid setup for beginners.

  o API Reference: Detailed specifications for /invoke, /batch, /stream, and /metadata endpoints.

  o Deployment Tutorials: Guides on integrating LangServe with Docker, Kubernetes, and CI/CD pipelines.

- Frequently Asked Questions: Solutions to common issues.

LangChain Documentation

- **URL**: LangChain Documentation

- **Overview**:

  - In-depth guide to building workflows with LangChain.

  - Includes tutorials, examples, and API references for core components.

- **Key Sections**:

  - Modular Components: Covers chains, memory, tools, and agents.

  - Tutorials: Step-by-step guides for building chatbots, question-answering systems, and more.

  - Integrations: Details on integrating LangChain with external APIs, databases, and libraries.

LangSmith Documentation

- **URL**: LangSmith Documentation

- **Overview**:

  - Documentation for monitoring and debugging LangChain workflows.

  - Explains how to enable tracing and visualize performance metrics.

E.2 Recommended Books, Courses, and Blogs

Books

1. **"LangChain in Action" by [Author Name]**

   - **Overview**: Comprehensive guide to using LangChain for AI workflows.

   - **Topics**: Workflow orchestration, advanced integrations, and real-world applications.

   - **Why Recommended**: Perfect companion to LangServe, providing in-depth context for building workflows.

2. **"Hands-On Machine Learning with Scikit-Learn, Keras, and TensorFlow" by Aurélien Géron**

   - **Overview**: Covers foundational machine learning and deep learning techniques.

   - **Topics**: End-to-end machine learning pipelines, model training, and deployment.

   - **Why Recommended**: Helps bridge gaps in ML understanding when integrating models with LangServe.

3. **"Building Machine Learning Pipelines" by Hannes Hapke and Catherine Nelson**

   - **Overview**: Explains how to construct scalable and maintainable ML pipelines.

   - **Topics**: Data ingestion, feature engineering, model deployment.

- o **Why Recommended**: Provides insights into integrating LangServe into larger AI pipelines.

Courses

1. **"LangChain for AI Developers" by [Platform Name]**

   - o **Platform**: [Coursera/Pluralsight/Udemy]

   - o **Overview**: Hands-on course for building LangChain workflows.

   - o **Why Recommended**: Focused specifically on LangChain and complements LangServe usage.

2. **"Deploying Machine Learning Models with Docker and Kubernetes" by [Platform Name]**

   - o **Platform**: Udemy

   - o **Overview**: Covers containerization and orchestration for ML applications.

   - o **Why Recommended**: Essential for deploying LangServe applications at scale.

3. **"Introduction to Cloud Computing for AI" by [Platform Name]**

   - o **Platform**: AWS Training/Google Cloud Training

   - o **Overview**: Explores cloud platforms and tools for AI deployment.

   - o **Why Recommended**: Provides a foundation for deploying LangServe applications on cloud platforms.

Blogs

1. **LangChain Blog**

   o **URL**: LangChain Blog

   o **Overview**: Covers updates, tutorials, and real-world use cases for LangChain.

   o **Why Recommended**: Frequently updated with practical insights for LangServe users.

2. **"AI Deployment Strategies" by [Author Name]**

   o **URL**: [Blog URL]

   o **Overview**: Explores best practices for deploying AI workflows.

   o **Why Recommended**: Provides actionable advice for LangServe applications.

3. **Towards Data Science**

   o **URL**: TDS

   o **Overview**: Articles on machine learning, AI, and deployment techniques.

   o **Why Recommended**: Covers a broad range of topics relevant to LangServe users.

E.3 Community Forums and GitHub Repositories

Community Forums

1. **LangChain Community Slack**

    o **URL**: Join Here

    o **Overview**: A dedicated Slack workspace for LangChain and LangServe discussions.

    o **Why Recommended**: Provides direct access to experts and peers for troubleshooting and idea-sharing.

2. **Reddit: r/MachineLearning**

    o **URL**: r/MachineLearning

    o **Overview**: Active community discussing AI trends, tools, and techniques.

    o **Why Recommended**: Engages with a diverse group of AI practitioners.

3. **Stack Overflow**

    o **URL**: Stack Overflow

    o **Overview**: Technical Q&A platform for coding and deployment issues.

    o **Why Recommended**: Search for or post questions about LangServe and related technologies.

GitHub Repositories

1. **LangServe**

   o **URL**: LangServe Repository

   o **Overview**: Official repository for LangServe with examples and documentation.

   o **Why Recommended**: Primary source for LangServe updates and community contributions.

2. **LangChain**

   o **URL**: LangChain Repository

   o **Overview**: Official LangChain repository with extensive examples and guides.

   o **Why Recommended**: Comprehensive resource for exploring LangChain integrations.

3. **Awesome AI Deployments**

   o **URL**: GitHub Repository

   o **Overview**: Curated list of tools and resources for deploying AI applications.

   o **Why Recommended**: Excellent starting point for exploring related technologies.

4. **FastAPI**

   o **URL**: FastAPI Repository

- Overview: Repository for FastAPI, a complementary tool for API development.

- Why Recommended: Useful for extending LangServe with custom endpoints.

This appendix equips you with an extensive collection of resources to deepen your understanding of LangServe and LangChain, as well as the broader ecosystem of AI deployment tools. By leveraging these official documentation, books, courses, blogs, forums, and repositories, you can stay up-to-date with the latest advancements, connect with the community, and refine your skills to build robust, innovative AI applications.

Appendix F: Example Code Repository

This appendix provides details on accessing the example code repository accompanying this book, along with step-by-step instructions on how to set up and run the provided examples. The repository contains complete, tested, and well-documented examples that align with the concepts discussed in each chapter.

F.1 Accessing the Book's Example Code

GitHub Repository

- **URL**: Example Code Repository

- **Repository Structure**: The repository is organized into directories corresponding to the book's chapters and appendices for easy navigation.

Directory	Description
/chapter-1/	Introduction to LangServe and LangChain examples
/chapter-2/	Getting started with LangServe setup and basics
/chapter-3/	API creation with LangServe
/chapter-4/	Deploying your first LangChain application
/chapter-5/	Scaling LangServe applications
/appendices/	Supplementary code snippets from

Directory	Description
	appendices

How to Clone the Repository

1. Install Git if you don't already have it:

   o   Download Git

2. Clone the repository to your local machine:

bash

```
git clone https://github.com/username/langserve-
book-examples.git
```

3. Navigate to the project directory:

bash

```
cd langserve-book-examples
```

F.2 How to Set Up and Run the Provided Examples

The example code is designed to be easy to set up and run. Below are detailed instructions to get started.

1. Prerequisites

Ensure that the following tools are installed on your system:

Tool	Minimum Version	Installation Command/Link
Python	3.9+	Download Python

Tool	Minimum Version	Installation Command/Link
Pip	Latest	Comes bundled with Python; upgrade using: pip install --upgrade pip
Docker (Optional)	20.10+	Download Docker
Git	Latest	Download Git

2. Setting Up the Environment

1. **Create a Virtual Environment**: It is recommended to use a virtual environment to manage dependencies.

bash

```
python -m venv env

source env/bin/activate   # For macOS/Linux

.\env\Scripts\activate    # For Windows
```

2. **Install Dependencies**: Navigate to the desired chapter directory and install the required Python libraries:

bash

```
pip install -r requirements.txt
```

3. Running the Examples

1. **Start the LangServe Application**: Navigate to the relevant example folder and run the application:

bash

```
python app.py
```

2. **Test the API**: Use tools like curl, Postman, or a web browser to interact with the running application.

Example: If you're running a chatbot example from /chapter-10/:

bash

```
curl -X POST http://localhost:8000/invoke \
    -H "Content-Type: application/json" \
    -d '{"query": "What is LangServe?"}'
```

Expected Response:

json

```
{
    "response": "LangServe is a deployment tool
for LangChain workflows."
}
```

4. Dockerized Examples

If Docker is installed, you can run the examples in a containerized environment for consistency.

1. **Build the Docker Image**: Navigate to the desired chapter folder and build the Docker image:

bash

```
docker build -t langserve-example .
```

2. **Run the Docker Container**:

bash

```
docker run -p 8000:8000 langserve-example
```

3. **Access the API**: The API will be available at http://localhost:8000.

5. Troubleshooting Common Issues

1. **Dependency Errors**:

   - Run the following to ensure all required packages are installed:

bash

```
pip install -r requirements.txt
```

2. **Port Already in Use**:

   - If you encounter this issue, stop the conflicting process or run the application on a different port:

bash

```
python app.py --port 8080
```

3. **Environment Issues**:

   - If you experience issues with your environment, recreate it:

bash

```
rm -rf env

python -m venv env

source env/bin/activate  # Or
.\env\Scripts\activate on Windows

pip install -r requirements.txt
```

Example Repository Structure

plaintext

langserve-book-examples/

├── chapter-1/

│   ├── app.py

│   ├── requirements.txt

│   └── README.md

├── chapter-2/

│   ├── app.py

│   ├── requirements.txt

│   └── README.md

├── chapter-10/

│   ├── chatbot_app.py
```
```

```
|   ├── requirements.txt
|   ├── Dockerfile
|   └── README.md
├── appendices/
|   ├── appendix-a/
|   |   ├── example_schema.py
|   |   └── README.md
|   └── appendix-f/
|       ├── docker_example.py
|       └── README.md
└── README.md
```

The example code repository is a valuable resource for learning and experimentation. With clear organization and comprehensive examples aligned to the book's chapters, it provides hands-on experience with LangServe and LangChain concepts. By following the setup and execution instructions, you can quickly replicate the examples and adapt them to your own projects. For further assistance, refer to the repository's README.md files or reach out via the community forums.

Chapter 21: Final Thoughts and Takeaways

This final chapter concludes the journey through the world of LangServe and LangChain. It recaps the key learnings from the book, encourages you to explore and innovate, and provides a forward-looking perspective on the evolving landscape of AI deployment technologies.

21.1 Recap of Key Learnings

1. The Power of LangServe for AI Deployment

- LangServe simplifies deploying LangChain workflows by automatically generating robust RESTful APIs and enabling real-time streaming capabilities.

- It reduces the complexity of moving AI applications from development to production, making it accessible for developers with limited DevOps expertise.

Key Features of LangServe:

- Built-in support for synchronous, batch, and streaming endpoints.

- Seamless integration with LangSmith for workflow monitoring and debugging.

- Extensibility for integrating custom tools, middleware, and external APIs.

2. Building and Scaling AI Applications

- **Chapters 2–5** focused on building and scaling LangServe applications:

    - **Setup**: A clear guide to installing and configuring LangServe.

    - **Deployment**: Walkthroughs on deploying LangChain workflows as scalable APIs.

    - **Scaling**: Techniques like autoscaling, caching, and load balancing for high-performance deployments.

Takeaway: LangServe's lightweight and modular architecture makes it suitable for both small-scale prototypes and enterprise-level applications.

3. Advanced Integration and Automation

- **Chapters 6–8** emphasized advanced topics like integrating LangServe with external tools, monitoring with LangSmith, and automating deployments with CI/CD pipelines.

- These chapters highlighted how to:

    - Use Docker and Kubernetes for containerized and orchestrated deployments.

    - Monitor workflow performance and debug errors using LangSmith.

    - Automate deployment processes to reduce manual overhead and ensure consistency.

Takeaway: Automation and monitoring are critical for maintaining robust and scalable LangServe applications.

4. Practical Use Cases

- **Chapters 9–12** explored real-world use cases of LangServe:

    - Chatbot APIs.

    - Knowledge retrieval systems.

    - Real-time streaming applications.

Takeaway: LangServe excels in practical applications that require natural language processing and AI-driven workflows, especially when paired with LangChain's modularity.

5. Preparing for Deployment

- **Chapters 13–16** provided detailed checklists and best practices for debugging, optimizing performance, and ensuring readiness for production environments.

Takeaway: Thorough preparation, including testing, monitoring, and security measures, ensures the success of AI deployments.

6. Future Trends and Innovation

- **Chapter 20** delved into the future of AI deployment technologies and how LangServe and LangChain will adapt to emerging trends like multi-modal AI, serverless computing, and edge deployments.

Takeaway: Staying informed about technological advancements and incorporating future-ready practices is essential for leveraging LangServe effectively.

21.2 Encouragement to Explore and Innovate

LangServe is more than just a deployment tool—it's a platform for experimentation, creativity, and innovation. Here are some ways to make the most of LangServe and LangChain:

1. Experiment with New Use Cases

- Combine LangChain workflows with external tools and APIs to develop unique applications.

- Examples:

  - A sentiment analysis API integrated with live social media feeds.

  - A personalized learning assistant that retrieves content based on user preferences.

2. Customize and Extend

- LangServe is designed to be extensible. Experiment with middleware for:

  - Custom authentication mechanisms.

  - Specialized data preprocessing or postprocessing.

3. Share Your Work

- Contribute to the growing LangChain and LangServe ecosystems by:

  - Publishing your workflows and middleware on GitHub.

o   Writing blogs or tutorials to share insights and best practices.

4. Collaborate Across Disciplines

- Collaborate with teams from various domains—business, education, healthcare—to identify problems that AI can solve.

- Example:

    o   A LangServe-powered chatbot for automating customer service in e-commerce.

5. Push Boundaries

- Explore advanced LangChain integrations:

    o   Use multi-modal models to handle text, images, and video in a single application.

    o   Deploy workflows at the edge for ultra-low-latency applications.

Encouragement: Your creativity and innovation can lead to breakthroughs in how AI is applied and deployed. With LangServe, you have the tools to bring your ideas to life.

21.3 A Look into the Evolving Landscape of LangServe and LangChain

LangServe and LangChain are rapidly evolving platforms, driven by a vibrant community and the demands of cutting-edge AI applications.

1. Future Features in LangServe

- **Multi-Modal Support**:

  - Expanding to handle workflows that combine text, images, and audio.

- **Serverless Integrations**:

  - Direct deployment to platforms like AWS Lambda and Google Cloud Functions.

- **Enhanced Security**:

  - Features like built-in OAuth2 support and advanced rate limiting.

2. LangChain's Evolution

- **Improved Modular Design**:

  - Simplifying the integration of third-party tools and services.

- **Expanded Ecosystem**:

  - Growing libraries and pre-built workflows for common tasks like summarization, translation, and sentiment analysis.

3. Trends Impacting LangServe

- **Edge Computing**:

  - Increasing demand for low-latency applications deployed closer to end-users.

- **Green Computing**:

- Optimizing deployments for reduced energy consumption and environmental impact.

- **AI Regulations**:

    - Tools to comply with emerging regulations for AI transparency and security.

4. Community Contributions

- **Open Source Innovations**:

    - Developers worldwide are contributing middleware, plugins, and integrations to extend LangServe's capabilities.

- **LangServe Community Forums**:

    - A thriving space for collaboration, troubleshooting, and idea exchange.

Final Message to Readers

LangServe empowers developers to transform complex AI workflows into production-ready applications with ease. It simplifies deployment, enhances scalability, and supports real-time capabilities—all while fostering innovation.

As you embark on your journey with LangServe and LangChain:

- Remember to **experiment boldly**.

- Stay curious and keep exploring the **latest advancements** in AI.

- Share your knowledge and contribute to the growing community of AI practitioners.

With LangServe, the possibilities are endless, and the future is yours to shape. Thank you for taking this journey, and here's to the remarkable AI applications you will create!

Acknowledgments

This book, *LangServe in Action: A Hands-on Guide to Deploying AI with LangChain*, is the culmination of collective efforts, insights, and support from various individuals and communities. It would not have been possible without their contributions.

Recognition of Contributors and Supporters

1. LangChain and LangServe Teams

- A heartfelt thank you to the teams behind LangChain and LangServe for creating such transformative tools. Your vision and innovation have made AI workflow development and deployment more accessible and streamlined.

- Special thanks to the developers and maintainers of LangChain and LangServe for their commitment to open-source principles, enabling a vibrant ecosystem of tools and resources.

2. Open-Source Contributors

- This book draws on the collective knowledge and expertise shared by the open-source community. The countless contributors who have enhanced LangChain, LangServe, and related libraries have played a vital role in making these technologies practical and versatile.

- Your blogs, repositories, and forums provided invaluable insights that shaped the content of this book.

3. Technical Reviewers and Advisors

- Gratitude goes to the technical reviewers who meticulously checked the examples, clarified concepts, and ensured accuracy throughout the chapters.

- Your feedback and guidance improved the book's quality and relevance.

4. Early Adopters and Beta Testers

- To the early adopters of LangServe and LangChain who shared their use cases, challenges, and feedback: your real-world experiences enriched this book with practical insights.

5. Educators and Advocates

- Educators, course creators, and AI advocates who have championed LangChain and LangServe have inspired this effort to make these tools more approachable to a broader audience.

6. Personal Support

- To family, friends, and colleagues who supported this project through its many iterations: your encouragement and belief made this journey possible.

Index

Keyword/Topic	Chapter	Page
API Key Authentication	Chapter 7	123
Apache Benchmark (AB)	Chapter 13, 15	178, 190

The Acknowledgments section highlights the collaborative spirit that brought this book to life, while the detailed Index ensures readers can easily navigate through the topics and examples discussed in the chapters. Together, they mark the culmination of an effort to make *LangServe in Action* an invaluable resource for developers, students, and professionals in the AI ecosystem.

www.ingramcontent.com/pod-product-compliance
Lightning Source LLC
LaVergne TN
LVHW080114070326
832902LV00015B/2582